Contemporary Glass

Contemporary Glass

black dog publishing
london uk

Contemporary Glass

Surface/Light

Installation

Note from the Editor
Blanche Craig

Glass is a medium entrenched in history. Some of the earliest examples of works in glass date back to the Byzantine era, in the guise of intricate and elaborate cut glass murals, in the stained glass windows produced in the Middle Ages and the—now-famous—work of the glass-blowers of Murano, Venice, in the thirteenth and fourteenth centuries. It was through the evolution of studio glass, however, initially proposed by the American ceramics professor Harvey Littleton in the mid-twentieth century, that innovations in glass practice really began to emerge. Since then, glass making techniques, and perceptions of the medium, have been challenged in greater and greater measure. This has led to current day practice that exceeds all boundaries of how glass is deployed by glass artists, erupting in discussion that both seeks to examine the shifting margins between glass and such genres as sculpture, installation and painting, as well as the complex relationship between the 'artist' and the 'craftsman'.

This volume does not seek to provide definitive answers to such issues, be an all-encompassing overview of the most prominent glass artists working today. It does, however, provide an entry point to the field, introducing the key themes prevalent in contemporary glass practice as well as some of the most influential and exciting glass artists working today.

Three essays, by Andrew Page, Heike Brachlow and Michael Petry, are featured throughout the book. In "A History of Sculptural Expression in Glass" Page traces the history of studio glass, from as early as Littleton's influence on the studio glass movement in America in the 1960s (and its subsequent impact on the rest of the Western world) through to the tradition of glass making in Venice and the impact of the sculptural glass installations by that most prolific of American glass artists, Dale Chihuly. Brachlow's "On Colour, Glass and Light", focuses on the seemingly limitless ways the properties of colour and light in glass have been exploited over time while, in "Through a Glass Darkly: Artists, Glass and Authorship", Petry explores the relationship between the artist and the craftsman, tying in concepts of 'authorship' and discussing how we can begin to define the resultant object from the collaboration between the two.

Over 60 glass artists are profiled in the book. Divided into four loose sections, "Vessel/Object", "Sculpture", "Surface/Light" and "Installation", a plethora of works are presented which, while assigned categories within the context of this volume, could easily transcend such boundaries. "Vessel/Object" introduces works that, while appearing to be traditional in form, soon reveal themselves to be complex and thought provoking works in their own right. Heike Brachlow, for example, sensitively employs the use of colour and light in her works, aiming to surpass perceptions of 'objecthood', while Suresh Dutt creates pieces whose very purpose is questioned through his manipulation of 'traditional' vessels. Kari Håkonsen takes this one step further, by creating objects which possess a hybrid sensibility, made manifest by their lace-like surfaces and their deconstruction of form.

"Sculpture" presents works that are more large-scale in nature and which begin to move away from the perceived functions of glass design. Beth Lipman, for example, makes grandiose still-lifes that echo the paintings of the Dutch masters of the seventeenth century, while Anne Brodie, creates dynamic sculptures that are purely abstract in form.

"Surface/Light" focuses on those works by artists that use glass as a surface on which to project both abstract and figurative forms and as a tool to manipulate and guide light. Lisa Cahill, for example, treats the surface of glass as a canvas on which to 'paint' and etch abstract landscapes, while Olafur Eliasson plays with the reflective nature of glass, resulting in Kaleidoscope-like effects. Anne Gant meanwhile, utilises glass to burn ambiguous shapes and patterns into other media, such as canvas and paper.

The last section, "Installation", introduces work that aims to initiate a dialogue with the spaces in which they are housed. Richard Box, for example makes huge outdoor installations, comprising rows of neon lights electromagnetically powered by the electricity lines overhead, whereas Tobias Rehberger utilises the traditional white cube space to suspend his ambitious glass and light installations, literally transforming such areas into rooms of illumination and reflection.

The glass artists featured in this volume are at the forefront of glass practice today. They continually challenge definitions of the medium and how it can be used. They deploy glass to reassert its position as one of the most exciting mediums today, exploit preconceptions and make works that seemingly defy categorisation. As such, they provide not only new parameters within which to consider glass today but have also set out a framework that future practitioners can engage with.

Vessel

Object

A History of Sculptural Expression in Glass

Andrew Page

Like other tales of great men who single-handedly changed the course of history, the oft-told saga of the birth of 'studio glass' celebrates a solitary founder, an American ceramics professor named Harvey Littleton who is widely credited with the liberation of molten glass from the factory. Like a modern-day Prometheus who stole the fiery magic of hot glass from industry and brought it to the art world, Littleton pioneered the development of small furnaces that allowed sculptors to work with the glowing, lava-like material in a studio setting. A visionary who foresaw the future for glass as a sculptural medium, Littleton became the spokesman for a self-proclaimed studio glass revolution that he billed as a new "movement" in art.

This legend of studio glass even has a time and place of birth—an eight day glass-blowing workshop Littleton organised in 1962, which took place at the Toledo Museum of Art in Ohio. This seminal event, held at an established art museum and led by a credentialed art professor, helped fuel glass' rapid acceptance in universities across America. Numerous articles in newspapers and magazines, as well as Littleton's subsequent travels to Europe, helped to make the impact of studio glass international.

Like most legends, however, there is more to the story. To start with, it was only with the help of others that Littleton was able to solve the technical challenges of blowing glass on a small-scale, and his was hardly the first use of glass as a material for sculptural expression.

Depending on how one defines it, artistic expression in glass can be traced back to its earliest uses in ancient times as adornment. If we apply the more contemporary idea of sculpture as an expression of ideas in the aesthetic arrangement of mass and volume, then one can point to a variety of efforts already underway in America and Europe—both by individuals and by large glass factories—to coax expressive, meaningful forms from glass.

For example, Louis Comfort Tiffany in America and Émile Gallé in France had pursued personal, purely sculptural forms in the material some 60 years before Littleton (though both Tiffany and Gallé employed skilled craftsmen to fabricate their designs). Probably the closest precursors to Littleton's artistic goals for glass were the efforts of progressive glasshouses in Sweden, The Netherlands, Finland, Czechoslovakia, and Italy. In the 1940s, 50s, and 60s, fine artists, architects, and designers were commissioned to design art objects that were blown or cast by highly trained workers and exhibited at international art and design expositions. Even outside the factories, a handful of individuals in Europe and America had experimented with a variety of glass techniques, including fusing and blowing glass, to directly express their ideas in the medium decades before Littleton's well-publicised breakthroughs.

Left:
Louis Comfort Tiffany,
circa 1808

Centre:
Tiffany and Company
Girl with Cherry Blossoms,
circa 1890

Right:
Émile Gallé
Vase, circa 1860

What was different about Littleton, beyond his undisputed powers of promotion, was his prodigious gift for inspiring followers and his talent for working within the system of higher education. His academic credentials as a professor of ceramics at the University of Wisconsin, Madison, gave glass immediate legitimacy and helped to speed up its adoption in university art programmes soon after his watershed Toledo workshop.

Littleton positioned himself as a rebel well-suited to the restless spirit of the era. By emphasising studio glass as a courageous breaking of centuries-old tradition, Littleton caught the cultural moment of 1960s America perfectly. He boasted of studio glass doing away with the long-standing separation of the person conceiving the work from the one actually making it, and he championed the potential for new expression possible only when a direct route was drawn between artist and material.

This breakthrough fit the cultural climate in America at the time, less than a decade after the death of Jackson Pollock, whose 'action-painted' spattered canvases liberated painting from the easel and paint from the brush, turning art into a record of performance. Abstract Expressionist painters such as Pollock had already inspired 'Studio Ceramic' artists such as Peter Voulkos who created rough-hewn and improvisational large-scale compositions, often in front of an audience. The resulting work was a record of spontaneity and raw expression as well as physical process of shaping clay with one's own hands. Molten glass—glowing with light, dangerously hot, subject to gravity and worked with an artist's breath—seemed the perfect next step in this search for pure expression. While studio glass encompasses many techniques of working with the medium, including casting, lampworking, and fusing, it was the theatre of blown glass that garnered the most attention in the early years.

In the 1960s, American universities—overflowing with a record number of students and led by administrators and faculty eager to embrace unconventional ways of doing things— began competing with one another to hire away Littleton's students in order to start glass programmes of their own. These young glass-blowing professors, some of whom had just themselves graduated, rolled up their sleeves and, with their students, hand-built the glass studios that sprung up in art schools around America.

The central role of the university in the growth of studio glass was a critical factor that would not be repeated outside of America. While a select few influential programmes did take root in university art programmes, such as those of the Royal College of Art in London and the Canberra Glass Workshop (part of the Australian National University), this was nothing in comparison to the popularity glass enjoyed in American academia. Their model of setting up working glass studios alongside fine arts programmes was not about to overturn the way glass was taught in many European countries. In Germany, Italy, Sweden, Denmark, the Czech Republic, and Austria, long-established educational programmes in glass offered vocational training to manual labourers, while designers were encouraged to study at the art academy and were not required to work with glass directly.

Despite maintaining this separation of maker and artist, the glass factories of Europe were quite progressive in their own efforts long before they came into contact with Littleton's revolutionary ideas. Venice, which had been for many centuries the world capital of fine glassmaking, had recovered from the onerous taxation during the years of rule by the

Hapsburg empire in the 1800s and, by the beginning of the twentieth century, the industry was revitalised. From the 1930s, Italian designers began to shift away from the historical revival that had, until then, been their focus, and began their ascent to the top tier of producers of mid-century modern glass objects. Designers such as Paolo Venini began to explore a new, decidedly modern, aesthetic that did away with superfluous decoration and referenced contemporary art in its use of more organic forms. Venetian glass masters such as Alfredo Barbini, who boasted a family pedigree that stretched back to the Middle Ages, had been experimenting with expressive shapes and colours clearly influenced by Mark Rothko, while the cooperative glasshouse, La Fucina degli Angeli (Forge of Angels), formed in 1950, began fabricating sculptures designed by some of the biggest names in contemporary art including Chagall, Picasso, Henry Moore, and Jean Cocteau.

In Sweden, where glass designers had been striving for Scandinavian restraint as part of the 'Beauty in Utility' movement, change was in the air by the mid-twentieth century. Radical new forms were being explored in the nation's design-forward glasshouses, such as Boda, where an aggressive young design director named Erik Höglund had been pushing against the predictability of Swedish glass in the late 1950s. This break with tradition accelerated with the arrival of Bertil Vallien, a Studio Ceramic sculptor who had lived in America and was hired by the glasshouses upon his return to his native country in the 1960s. Vallien, who had visited some of the earliest American studio glass artists, linked the raw energy of the studio glass and Studio Ceramics movements with the highly developed technical skills available at the glass factories in Sweden.

Meanwhile, on the other side of the Iron Curtain in Soviet-era Czechoslovakia, the long-established factory system for Bohemian glass provided a rare outlet for artistic freedom and abstraction, drawing sculptors to the medium. Cast-glass sculptures that built on pre-war Czech Cubism, yet employed the so-called utilitarian medium of glass, flourished most notably in works by Stanislav Libensky and Jaroslova Brychtova who influenced a generation of Czech sculptors to work in glass. Czech cast-glass sculpture became well-known through international design expositions and would later have a major impact on American studio glass makers who would begin to experiment with casting, blowing and work in larger scale.

While most European glass producers maintained their factory systems, and the division of creative and manual roles, the model of the artist and maker being one and the same person did find foothold in some European countries. As such it was largely encouraged by the work of individuals who had come into direct contact with Littleton—most notably Erwin Eisch in Germany and Sybren Valkema in The Netherlands. Each became a leading proponent of the radical new approach to creative glassmaking in their native countries, and each played a role in bringing a new, rough-hewn improvisational aesthetic as spontaneous as the process of glass-blowing to their own country.

Erwin Eisch was born into a Bavarian family of glass producers and went on to study fine art at university. Upon returning home to the family glass factory, he began exploring sculptural concepts in molten glass that broke existing aesthetic restrictions with asymmetrical, expressive forms. Littleton stumbled upon Eisch's work during a visit to Germany the same year as his famous 1962 Toledo Workshop, and eagerly sought out the maker. Littleton and Eisch became lifelong friends, and the inspiration was mutual. Encouraged by Littleton's success in America, Eisch would become the German champion of studio glass, which would develop a following in Germany with little support from the academic or vocational schools. In 1987, Eisch established the International Summer Academy Bild-Werk Frauenau to help to crystallise the efforts of European artists working in glass by providing a forum to share techniques and to socialise, much as they had been doing at summer schools such as Pilchuck or Haystack in America for decades.

Opposite left:
Z1, 2007
Blown free form glass
Image courtesy of Zest
Gallery. Photograph by
Adam Aaronson.

Opposite centre:
Z Series, 2007
Blown free form glass.
Image courtesy of Zest
Gallery. Photograph by
Adam Aaronson.

Opposite right:
Z2, 2007
Blown free form glass.
Image courtesy of Zest
Gallery. Photograph by
Adam Aaronson.

Meanwhile, in The Netherlands, Sybren Valkema had built the first small studio furnace in a European art school in 1965. Before meeting Littleton, Valkema had been employed as a designer at the Leerdam glass factory, and had been looking for ways to make the technology of the glass furnace available for individual artists. He found the answer when he attended the 1964 World Congress of Craftsmen in New York City, where he had been sent by the Dutch Ministry of Culture. Having observed the furnace that Littleton was using to demonstrate small-scale glass-blowing, Valkema returned home determined to break down the factory wall. In 1965, Valkema set up the glass furnace at the Gerrit Rietveld Academie in Amsterdam. In 1969, he would work with a curator from a museum in Rotterdam to organise a travelling exhibition of studio glass that would exhibit work by American studio glass artists and help bring this creative approach to a wider audience.

In Britain, on the arrival of Littleton's former student, Sam Herman, in 1964, the influence of Littleton's approach to studio glass had also begun to emerge. After setting up a small glass furnace at the Royal College of Art in London, Herman was hired as research fellow and would lead the College's glass department until 1974, giving rise to a small but influential group of artists working directly with glass. Herman also set up a small glass furnace at the Stourbridge College of Art and Design near Birmingham, where Keith Cummings led a glass programme for decades and gave special emphasis to the kiln-forming of glass. It is notable that, in those places where studio glass found support in Europe, there was always greater openness to all methods of working with the material—from kiln-forming to lampworking—while blown glass dominated in America until the 1980s. After his time in England, Herman went on to Australia where he built one of the country's first glass-blowing facilities in Adelaide in the mid-1970s. In 1983, German-born Klaus Moje, arrived in Australia to set up the Glass Workshop at Canberra, now a part of the Australian National University system.

While studio glass managed to find a home in a handful of institutions in Britain, The Netherlands, Germany, and Australia, other countries, such as Sweden, the Czech Republic, or Italy, were not about to make significant changes to longstanding factory apprenticeship systems. Yet, even in these countries, the studio glass model would produce lasting changes. Many individuals working in glasshouses were inspired by the new approach to glass in America, and would break out of their subordinate roles as fabricators and launch highly successful careers of their own.

Some of these individuals, such as Anne Wolff in Sweden, Frantisek Vizner in Czechoslovakia, or Lino Tagliapietra in Venice, began to travel to America to participate in

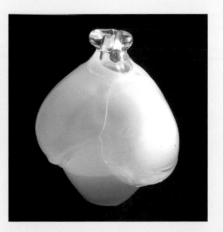

lectures and symposiums in the late 1970s. These highly trained glass craftsmen, who were liberated by the studio glass ethos, began to share their techniques and expertise at a number of emerging glass symposiums in America, and later, in Europe. The most important of these was the Pilchuck Glass School in the American state of Washington. Started by celebrated glass artist, Dale Chihuly, in 1971, Pilchuck provided a forum for artists to share technical knowledge, and it was the place where the studio glass movement coalesced. Along with the summer programmes at craft centres such as Penland, Haystack, as well as non-profit arts centres for glass such as the New York Experimental Glass Workshop, Pilchuck became a regular stop for those glass masters visiting from Europe and Asia. The American studio glass artists were hungry for technical knowledge and were eager to absorb skills gained under traditional glass factory systems.

During the early years of studio glass, artists sought to break with the symmetry and beautiful surfaces of factory-made glass with highly personal, thick-walled organic forms. The distinguishing feature of much of the earliest work in glass is its crudeness, which has its own expressive power but also evidences a lack of technical skill. With the focus on the individual maker, studio glass presented a clean break with tradition. The pioneers of the movement were happy to start from scratch even though there were limitations to the complexity of the objects they could make. This began to change, however, when they were exposed to the work of highly trained glass-makers from Europe whose skills had been perfected over centuries of apprenticeship learning.

Over time the studio glass field expanded, skills improved, and orthodoxies were abandoned as individual artists devoted themselves to learning time-honoured techniques. Such evolution of studio glass is embodied by the example of Paul and Dante Marioni, the father and son who are both prominent American artists working with glass. Paul Marioni was a pioneer in the early generation of studio glass and his work is earthy, humorous, and symbolic; often with a weighty volume. His son, Dante Marioni, has taken a completely different path, and his work is as light and refined as glass can be blown. (It was after seeing pieces blown by Italian maestro Lino Tagliapietra at Pilchuck that Dante devoted himself to mastering traditional Venetian techniques). The differences between the two could not be starker, and are a perfect lens for reflecting some of the changes that took place in studio glass between the 1970s and 90s.

When he started blowing glass in 1980, Dante Marioni had no interest in pursuing his father's heavy, sculptural style. Having started blowing glass while still a teenager, the younger Marioni was able to develop extremely refined skills which he has employed to create his signature outsized vessels that have defied preconceptions of the scale of

blown glass. His work marries the finest Italian technique with a bold American vision of limitless possibilities.

This rise in technical skills has led to a more complex landscape than in the early days of studio glass, when the emphasis was on unifying the role of artist and fabricator. It has become routine now for many highly skilled glass-blowers to work for other glass artists, most prominently in the case of Chihuly who employs up to 90 workers in the production of his blown-glass assemblage art. Well-known contemporary artists who choose to employ glass—most prominent among them Robert Rauschenberg, Jim Dine, and KiKi Smith— often have their work fabricated by some of the most technically accomplished studio glass artists working today (although such fabricators are rarely credited). Though this has allowed glass art to be shown in major museum exhibitions, it has also contributed to a sense of divide between glass as a so-called craft versus a fine-art.

Glass artists in America—like ceramics artists—have struggled for acceptance by the larger art world, which often remains suspicious of an intense focus on material. Those artists working with the medium of glass must often overcome the preconception that their work is first and foremost materials-based, and that it is therefore not concerned with larger conceptual or political issues. At least in America, where a network of galleries specialising in art made from glass has developed, the parallel universe of fine art galleries and glass galleries is often discussed in plaintive terms. Despite the use of glass by major artists, or the successes of individual glass artists such as Chihuly, the majority of artists working in glass struggle for wider acceptance. In Europe, where the strict separation between so-called craft and so-called fine art is not as strict, this has been less of a burning issue, though it should be noted that the market for art made from glass is not as developed. As a result, the world's largest exposition of art from craft media, which is known as Sculptural Objects Functional Art (SOFA) and is held in the American city of Chicago, has started to draw artists working in glass from as far away as Japan, Israel, Australia, and Eastern Europe. This annual event brings together mostly American collectors and a broad range of artists who are advancing studio glass far beyond what even Littleton might have imagined. The number of galleries selling glass, and museums exhibiting it, is far greater within America than outside of it. It is fitting, in some ways, that studio glass remains most commercially viable in the country where it was first founded.

Above:
Jim Dine
*Twelve Pierced
Vessels*, 2000
Glass and found objects,
81.9 x 546.1 x 27.9 cm.
© Jim Dine/Wetterling
Gallery, ARS, NY and
DACS, London 2008.

Opposite Left:
*Red and Yellow Acorn
Vases*, circa 2000

Opposite right:
Paul Marioni
The Kiss, 2006
Kiln-cast glass,
10 x 38 x 23 cm,
Photograph by
Russell Johnson.

Heike Brachlow

Heike Brachlow is an artist whose colourful and evocative works seek to defy traditional perceptions of 'objecthood'. Her practice draws inspiration from architecture, geometry and the human condition, resulting in works that are understated yet poignant, fragile but robust. Brachlow communicates such conditions through the manipulation of colour and light in her glass works, using age-old techniques that have evolved over decades, as well as striving to create new and innovative ways to employ colour in her work.

Brachlow's objects have the dual purpose of appearing static while also possessing kinetic potential (works such as *Mirror Movement I*, 2006, move when touched, for example), while forms that are seemingly tough could collapse at any moment (as is evidenced in pieces such as *Barrier*, 2006).

A PhD student at the Royal College of Art, Brachlow's research focuses on light and form in solid glass sculpture. An interest that inevitably feeds into her artistic practice, Brachlow is particularly influenced by the work of Czech glass artists—the cubist creations of Stanislav Libensky and Jaroslava Brychtová, for example—and also seeks to address the difficulty of innovation in colour glass because the hues available to artists are not finite. As a result Brachlow has begun to invent her own glass colour, aiming to achieve the most luminous and transparent results possible.

Brachlow has exhibited widely, including Nadania Idriss Contemporary Art and Photography, Berlin, 2008, the Crafts Council Showcase at the Victoria and Albert Museum, London, 2007, the Commission for Best of British Industry Awards: Innovation in Industry, Tate Modern, London, 2007, as well as the Pilchuck Glass School Annual Auction, Seattle, London and the British Glass Biennale 2006 Ruskin Glass Centre, 2006.

1

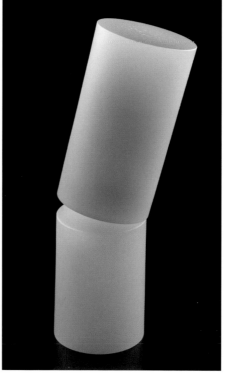

2

1 *On Reflection II*, 2006
Cast glass,
21 x 23.5 cm.
Photograph by
Silvain Deleu.

2 *Waiting IV*, 2008
Cast glass,
16.5 x 51 cm.
Photograph by
Ester Segarra.

3 *Mirror Movement I*, 2006
Cast glass,
16 x 30 cm.
Photograph by
Simon Bruntnell.

4

4 *Fire Trilogy*, 2004
Kiln-cast glass,
27 x 15 cm.
Photograph by
Simon Bruntnell.

5 *Orbit Series I*, 2008
  Kiln-cast glass,
  28 x 60 x 9.5 cm.
  Photograph by
  Ester Segarra.

Matthew Curtis

Matthew Curtis is one of Australia's most prominent glass artists. In 2003 he was awarded the National Sculpture Prize at the National Gallery of Australia and he continues to showcase his work in prestigious galleries across the world.

After training under Robert Wynne at the Denizen Glass Design studios, in Manly, Australia, Curtis helped to build a hot glass workshop, where he continued to work on his own projects as well as collaborating with others (Ben Edols, Kathy Elliot, Bettina Visentin and Richard Whiteley). In 1996 Curtis was selected as a finalist for the prestigious RFC Glass Prize as well as being awarded the People's Choice Prize.

Curtis developed his technique and style over a number of years, while assisting in a number of other large-scale collective projects with a diverse range of international glass artists, such as Dale Chihuly. His own work is often ambitious in scale and form. He enjoys the tension created between the fragility of his materials and a top-heavy design—often reaching up to one metre in height—which threaten to topple over and smash, mimicking the tentative balance between presence and absence.

His signature curved *Thorax* and *Carapace* works straddle a thin line between minimalist contemporary architecture and objects to be found in the natural world. There is something slightly menacing about these forms, despite their smooth, polished curves and surfaces. As Curtis explains:

> These pieces are designed to maximise some of the most alluring attributes of the material, whilst conceptually using the perforated surface/skin of the form in order to glimpse the interior. This allows the unseen to be experienced, alluding to so many aspects of our experiences where there is more to be seen and understood than is initially apparent.

The methods of production are complicated, deriving from various moulding techniques. Curtis initially melts colours in a pot furnace to create different tints. He then blows the components of the sculpture in a series of steel moulds, leaving a trapped pocket of air within. When assembled these parts:

> Create a veiled aesthetic with an internal structure of colours that fade and gather intensity depending on the thickness of the glass. So too, the envelope of air effects our experience of the coloured glass, creating a diaphanous structure within.

This process of layering is essential to the personal mythology that lies at the heart of his work; "childhood discovery" and nature.

1

2

1 *Constructed Cherry Bowl*, 2006
Blown glass interior bowl, surrounded by mantle of float glass, stainless steel rim, 22 x 56 x 56 cm.
Photograph by Rob Little.

2 *Scalloped Ivory* (detail), 2008
Blown overlaid glass, lathe worked, 67 x 23 x 9 cm.

3 *One Bar Red*, 2005
Blown overlaid glass, engraved and lathe worked, 84 x 25 x 10 cm.
Photograph by Rob Little.

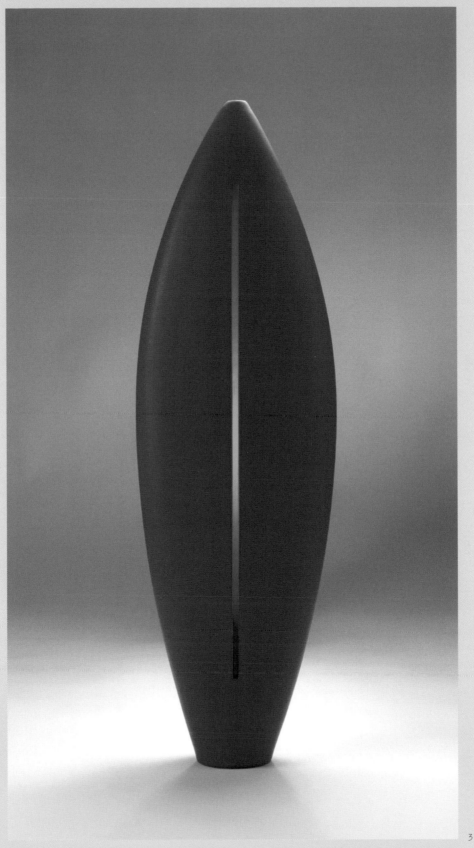

Suresh Dutt

Suresh Dutt is an artist who aims to turn perceptions of the glass medium upside down. He is particularly fascinated by its physical properties and how they can suggest form and structure in certain spaces. The result is an oeuvre where glass vessels are mutated, seemingly flat surfaces are comprised by a multitude of layers, and colour emerges and disappears from varying perspectives. In these works, optical qualities are pushed to their limits, often with surprising effects.

Dutt's combines hand blown, cast and flat glass with various decorative techniques in his work. He explores

the optical qualities of glass through the construction of form and space using colour and transparency to define contours and visual density [and utilise] complex geometries and optical effects to expose abstract qualities such as volume, containment and suspension.

Dutt exhibits extensively in Europe and Asia, and has acquired numerous awards

as well as residency opportunities from such organisations as the Arts Council England and the Crafts Council. Previous exhibitions include Sothebys, Crafts Council and Victoria & Albert Museum in London, Museo de Arte en Vidrio de Alcorcon in Madrid, Axis Gallery in Tokyo and Manchester Art Gallery in Manchester. In 2005, he was selected by Professor Marian Karel to receive the Arts Council England/Visiting Arts/British Council 'International Artists Fellowship' to the Academy of Art Architecture & Design (VSUP) in Prague.

1

1 *Device TRG*, 2002
Hand-blown glass,
graduated transparent
grey incalmo, cut
and polished,
30 cm in diameter.

2 *DS Bowl*, 2002
Hand-blown glass, opaque
black with opaque yellow
interior, cut
and polished,
25 cm in diameter.

3 *DS FLZ*, 2002
Hand-blown glass, double
layer of opaque ivory,
cut and polished,
30 cm in diameter.

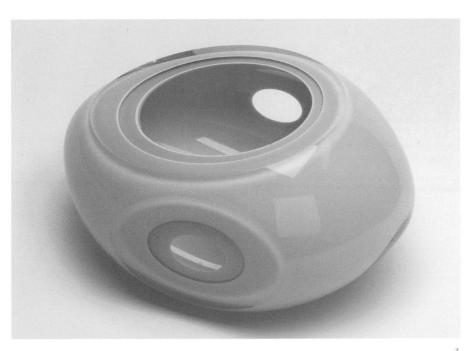

3

Anne Haavind

Haavind's abstract approach to glass is inspired by the Oslo artist colony she grew up in, while the geometry of her sculptures reflects both the Nordic landscape of her youth and natural and classical forms drawn from her later travels. The defining characteristics of her sculptures are their scale and geometry, as she explores the forms that glass creates naturally and manipulates its material qualities—transparency, cut and colour—into sculptural forms with hypnotic optical qualities.

The shapes she makes are captured rather than planned. Working with the still-warm glass, she melts and shapes it simultaneously, holding it at certain angles to create the right dimensions and stopping the process at exactly the moment when the perfect shape is achieved.

Haavind's *Unica* sculptures turn the unpredictabity of glass into a creative tool. Instead of aiming to control the difficult glass-making process, the medium is employed to generate a series of forms which are all unique. The natural movement of warm glass dictates the forms, their fluid shapes and the way the colours and textures of the different types of glass, blend.

Each piece in the *Unica Series* is conceived as a series of technical sketches that Haavind uses to illustrate her artistic vision to a team of glass-makers. "After several years we have developed a mutual understanding", she says, "and the work process is both a dance and a very physical workout". Thereafter, the objects are sawn and polished into their final form. "Glass is a floating and rounded form", says Haavind, "so it is interesting to cut it, to treat it like ice".

Since the 1980s, Haavind has become increasingly interested in the environmental possibilities of using glass, as the production process is both lead-free, and pays particular attention to working conditions and environmental impact. She is currently looking into future projects using recycled crystal.

1

1 *Plata Royal*, 2006
Clear crystal
glass, pigment,
55 cm in diameter.

2 *Retro Line*, 2007
Clear crystal glass,
transparent opac pigment.
All photographs by
Chris Harrison.

Kari Håkonsen

Kari Håkonsen is one in a growing number of artists who fuses traditional glass-blowing with new and innovative techniques, where the process of making is just as integral to her work as the finished object. Her practice centres largely on the (perceived) female tradition of making and other signifiers of femininity. This concern became particularly prevalent in the series Insertion, 2007, and in her Othilie vases and bowls, also 2007, which comprise a diverse range of both functional and non-functional objects that the artist makes in freehand glass and subsequently carves, sandblasts, and engraves with patterns and designs appropriated from vintage crochet and antique lace.

In the Insertion works, in particular, all reference to function is abandoned. What is left behind is a series of works that appear to decompose before the viewer's eyes, leaving barely a trace of the process by which they were realised. In such works, intricate detail is also revealed, hinting at a material whose limits have seemingly been stretched beyond recognition.

Håkonsen is also interested in the potential glass proffers to preserve certain elements and how it can become precious or valued in its own right. These concerns are also implicated in the Insertion Series—whereby the artist sources the textiles imprinted on its surfaces for next to nothing, and then destroys them in the process of making.

In so doing, it is the objects themselves that bear the mark of antiquity and value.

Based in Norway, Håkonsen is cited as one of the country's most influential young artists. She has exhibited worldwide, including exhibitions in Norway, Sweden, Britain, The Netherlands and America and has work in the collections of the Statsbygg for The Norwegian Ambassy in Berlin, The Museums of Arts and Crafts, Oslo, and The National Library, Norway.

1

2

1 *Insertion*, 2007
Glass, blown and
sandblasted,
43 cm in length.

2 *Insertion*, 2007
Glass, blown and
sandblasted,
32 cm in length.

3 *Othilie*, 2007
Glass, blown and
sandblasted,
50 x 22 cm.
All photographs
by Siri Möller.

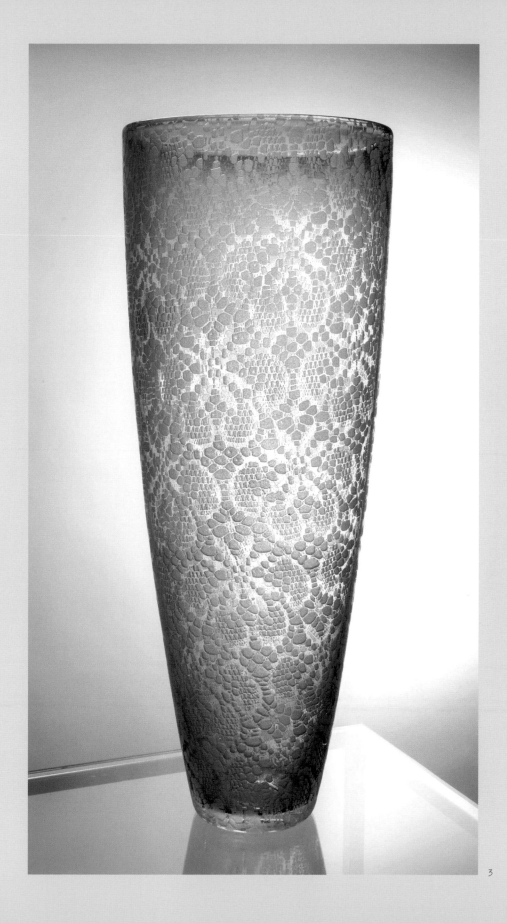

3

Lena Hansson

Lena Hansson's glass compositions are at once playful and emotive. Bright, energetic colours combine with functional objects (whether they be human limbs, lightbulbs, vessels or building blocks) and light shines on and through them, resulting in a life-like quality that contradicts their seemingly static nature. Hansson is interested in the diversity of forms that can be created from glass, thus resulting in a diverse oeuvre that comprises glassware, sculpture, stained glass and wall-mounted 'paintings' in two-dimensions. Similarly, she is not limited by form, producing pieces that range from figurative objects such as birds and bones through to transcending into pure abstraction.

Hansson also plays with surface and texture in her work—a pair of vases are treated with a woodgrain facade, for example. More recent forays into the medium see Lansson play with the dual characteristics of fragility and strength that glass possesses, resulting in robust compositions of colour-tinted block, architectural pieces that are literally 'built' while still holding the potential for collapse (one push and they would and break apart).

Hansson qualified in industrial design at the National Handicraft and Industrial School in Norway and has worked as a designer for Hadeland's glassworks since the early 1990s. She is represented by the Industrial Arts Museum in Oslo and frequently exhibits in Norway. In 1996 Hansson received the Norwegian Design Council's price for Good Design.

1

1 *Untitled*, circa 2000   2 *Untitled*, circa 2000

Joseph Harrington

Joseph Harrington juxtaposes a plethora of opposites in his work. The notions of solid and liquid; strength and weakness; hot and cold; past and present are expertly explored throughout the body of work as are the transitional phases between these states. Harrington admits he is "fascinated with turning one thing into another, the reaction of materials and energies acting upon each other".

In keeping with the preoccupation with transient states ice—the most extreme state of water—is used as a cast for Harrington's glass sculptures. In essence, ice is a temporal material, only retaining its form at subhuman temperatures and transient in nature (its only certainty being that it will melt).

Utilising age-old processes, the ice is eroded and sculpted with salt. These 'lost' processes are artistically employed and the ice is cast into the searing hot glass, forever immortalised in the medium through degenerative transition. This thawing of ice to Harrington, "provides a physical time frame to work within, heightening the importance of artistic judgment and decision-making". The knife-like realisation of the form is rendered almost passive as the aggressive, streamlined, sharp sensibility literally melts away. The resultant forms seem to become impotent victims of attack, rather than protagonists, as their stabbing ability is disabled by outside forces. The aesthetic of Harrington's work is reminiscent of the found object—that of

an archaeological dig—giving each viewer the sense of discovering an ancient relic from a bygone era. This simply reiterates the primitive processes employed to initially construct the sculpture: ice and salt.

The physicality of glass mimics that of ice but with one major difference. Despite their heat related loss of form and their genuine fragility the sculptures rendered in glass remain strong, overcoming the constraints of their previously temperature controlled existence; these sculptures refuse to melt.

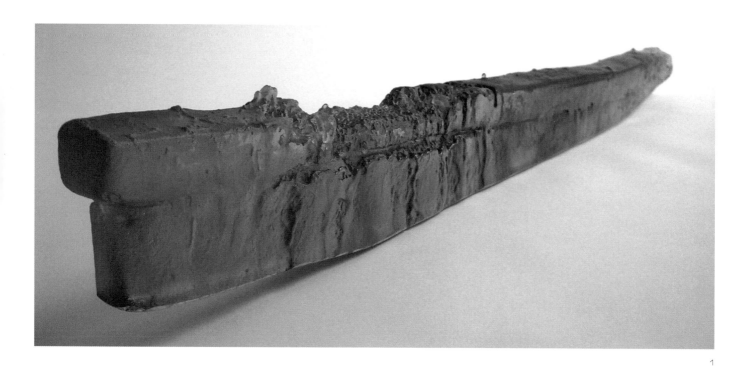

1

1 *Ice Bar*, 2006
Kiln-cast glass, lost
ice process,
82 x 10 x 5 cm.

2 *Wedge*, 2006
Kiln-cast glass, lost
ice process,
29 x 22 x 7 cm.
Photograph by
Colin Mills.

3 *Bent Girder*, 2007
Kiln-cast glass,
85 x 28 x 8 cm.

2

3

Jamie Harris

Jamie Harris is a glass artist and designer who lives and works in New York. Having studied at such renowned glass schools as The Pilchuck Glass School, the Rhode Island School of Design, and the Corning Museum of Glass, Harris cites as his influence as Dante Marioni, Josiah McElheny, Benjamin Moore and Kathy Eliot; some of the most iconic glass artists working today.

Harris' practice is distinguished by his evocative use of colour and design, making sculptures and objects that are playful and functional in equal measure. Works such as *Incendary*, 2005, part of the *Incalmo Series*, epitomise this approach. Here, kaleidoscope colours are layered one atop another, creating a multitude of tones and levels of opacity in blown and carved glass. In his continual exploration of the possibilities of colour, Harris not only refers to the traditional glass works produced by Venetian glass-blowers, but also to American modernist painting.

Harris frequently uses carving in his practice as a device to deconstruct traditional vessel shapes. The resultant objects can be found in series such as *Zip Series*, 2007, a combination of seemingly functional objects like vases and plates, and *Zip Block Installation*, one of many abstract wall mounted compositions. Here aggressive carving works to expose and contrast colour with "balance and symmetry".

Harris moves further into abstraction with *The Colour Field Series*. Here, layers of glass are fused and then carved to reveal striking compositions which look more like painting than glass work.

Harris places great importance on the processes involved in making his works, relying on a large number of specialist glass makers to bring his concepts to fruition. He prefers this collaborative approach to working alone, citing it as an integral part of his practice: "The assemblage of collected talent yields a higher degree of intensity and creative output than could be achieved in the glass studio by working alone." This multiplicitous approach to making is more than evident in the layered and complex works that the artist makes.

1

2

1 *Incendiary (incalmo orb series)*, 2005
Blown and carved glass, 45.7 x 45.7 x 20.3 cm.
Photograph by George Ermol.

2 *Zip Block Installation*, 2007
Blown and carved glass, 121.9 x 30.5 x 17.8 cm.
Photograph by James Dee.

3 *Cut Out Installation*, 2007
Solid worked and carved glass, 114.3 x 30.5 x 15.2 cm.
Photograph by James Dee.

Karl-Oskar Karlsson

Karl-Oskar Karlsson is a young Swedish designer who creates minimalist, beautiful and organic designs with a contemporary twist. "As I am educated in both art and design" he explains:

I search for new combinations with both the design process and my own expression. I work with different materials to [create] contrasts and different categories of products to [provide] new ways of using the object.

Karlsson's practice is essentially concept-led, enabling him to set a mental map at the outset and approach the design of an object from diverse perspectives. During this process, he employs contrasting styles, materials and techniques and fuses the retro with the modern, the conceptual with the decorative.

Karlsson's most recent work is the internationally recognised *Combine Series*, which conflates glass and wood; both natural materials present in the Kingdom of Crystal, a Southern Swedish geographical area. The contrast created in such fusion of materials gave new life to each one used. "The warm, soft, changeable wood contrasts with the hard, shiny and fragile glass. The shapes were held to classical vases to allow the materials receive more attention", Karlsson claims. "My future work will be a continuation of finding new expressions in combinations." This has resulted in a continuation in Karlsson's practice of transcending the borders of art and design, and of challenging processes of making and the way that objects might look and be used.

Karl-Oskar Karlsson studied in the Kalmar School of Design in Sweden, where he graduated with a Bachelor of Arts and a MA in Product Design. He has exhibited widely in Sweden and Europe and has participated in group shows such as the International Glass Design, Between Art and Design and Archive for Swedish Design. He is currently a member of Kalmar's School of Design application jury.

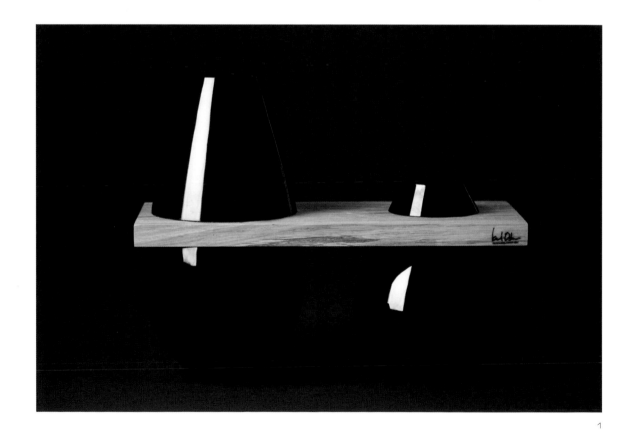

1

1 *Duo*, circa 2006
Black glass and oak,
41 x 18 x 32 cm.

2 *Base*, 2006
Black glass and oak,
17 x 32 cm.

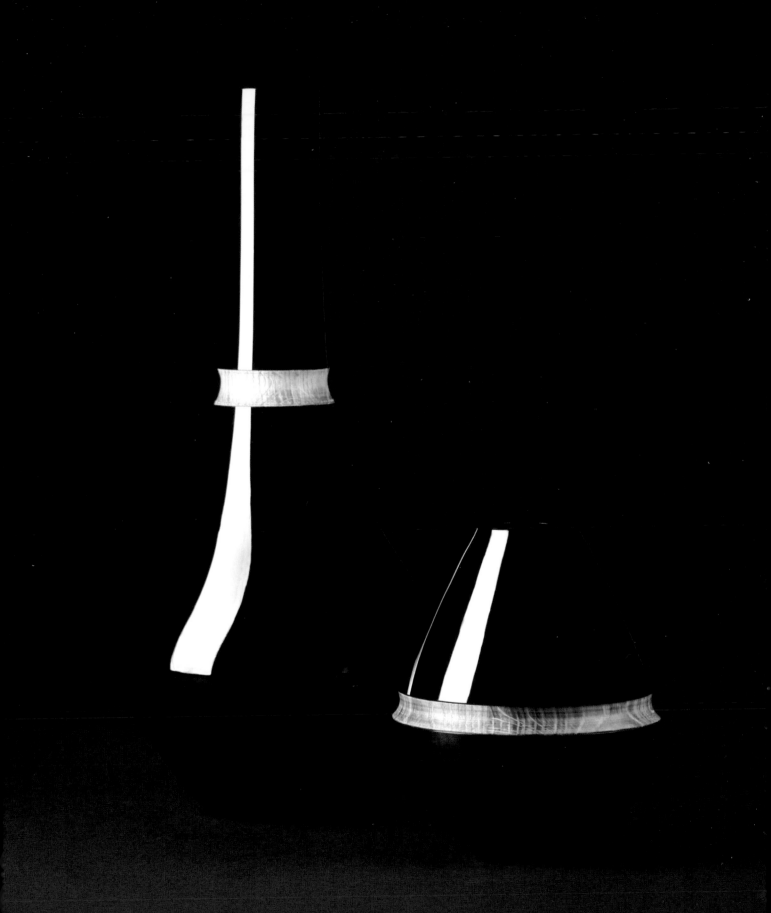

4

3 *Stripe Unique and*
Stripe Small, 2006
Black glass and oak,
22 x 49 cm (Stripe
Unique) and 20 x 16 cm
(Stripe Small).

4 *Tiger*, 2006
Black glass and oak,
37 x 22 cm.

Jeremy Lepisto

Jeremy Lepisto uses simple glass forms as a starting point, upon which he etches a variety of narrative forms, often in series. Lepisto has co-founded (together with his wife and partner Mel George) Studio Ramp LLC, a custom kiln forming fabrication studio that translates artists' and architects' designs into glass, from concept through to completion. This interest in architectural forms runs throughout Lepisto's practice, whereby he frequently chooses to depict scenes from the built environment in his series-based glass etchings.

Lepisto hand-renders the images in his work (without the aid of any special equipment or preparation), and refers to a large visual vocabulary, which gives rise to a truly distinctive aesthetic throughout his work. The subjects of the works are inspired by relationships between individuals or people and places, with a particular emphasis on the narrative of the familiar, yet non-specific, urban space. The result is a strange tension between the static permanence of the glass medium and the ephemeral nature of the scenes depicted, creating a disjunction between form and content that opens up the work to a wider interpretation of the modern experience. Lepisto extends this uncertain mood by the colour and aesthetic forms typical of his work, trapping architectural and social information in sepia-tones between thick panes of etched glass, rendering the images themselves simultaneously familiar but forever unattainable.

Born in Fort Belvoir, Virginia, Lepisto is now based in Portland, Oregon, and has exhibited widely in both group and solo exhibitions across America. Lepisto is the recipient of the Hauberg Fellowship and Alfred University Pilchuck Glass School Scholarship.

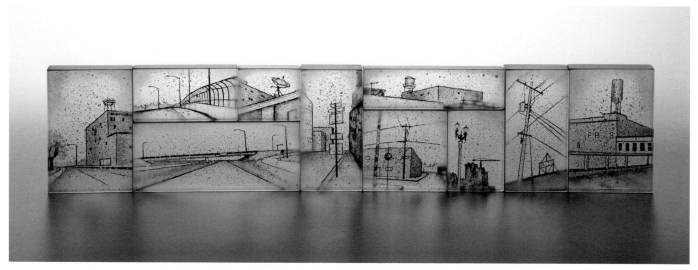

1

1 *Along the Way* (from the *Building Block Series*), 2007
Bullseye glass with Paradise Paint and Bullseye powder imagery, 72 x 14.5 x 4 cm.

2 *Makes the Man* (from the *Slider Series*), 2006
Bullseye glass with Paradise Paint and Bullseye powder imagery with fabricated aluminium, 51 x 12.5 x 2 cm.

3 *Available Connection* (from the *Bridge Series*), 2004
Bullseye sheet glass with Paradise Paint imagery, 89 x 10 x 2.5 cm.
All photographs by Paul Foster.

2

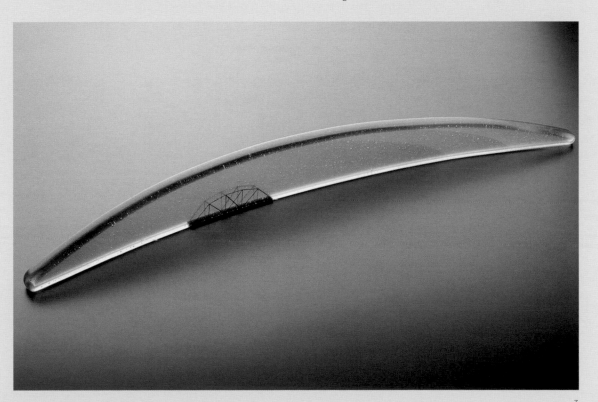

3

Ingrid Nord

Norwegian artist Ingrid Nord has been exploring the technique of blown glass since 2000, using a variety of cold working techniques, such as cutting and sandblasting. Nord decorates blown glass vases with sandblasted patterns of faces, cityscapes and other urban imagery. She explains:

> I wanted to present this theme through an expression that did not lose its integrity by the limitations of the image making process, being strengthened by the characteristics of the glass.

Her latest series of blown glass objects captures the 'organised chaos' of the city landscape. By reducing images of urbanity to strongly defined lines and patterns of shadow and light, she encapsulates a sense of noise and movement within a highly structured landscape.

Inspired by the stark contrasts of graphic art and the opposition between light and darkness, Nord creates her images using *graal*. A technique originally developed from overlay glass by Knut Bergqvist and Simon Gates in 1916 in the glass producing area of Smaland in southern Sweden, *graal* involves working on different layers of glass in stages to produce a three-dimensional effect, without diminishing the integrity of the image. It counts as one of the most demanding techniques glass-blowers can attempt. Nord takes this traditional technique to new levels, incorporating contemporary, cutting edge imagery in her ouevre.

Since graduating from Edinburgh College of Art with a Bachelor of Fine Arts in 2005, Nord has undertook several placements in studios in Norway, Australia and Scotland. Ingrid received several prices for her *Urban Life Series* in 2005. In 2007, she was selected for two juried exhibitions: Young Glass in Denmark and Triennalen in Oslo. She now lives and works in Bergen, Norway, where she has recently opened a workshop with three other artists.

1

2

1&2 Glass objects from the *Urban Life Series*, 2005 Blown glass sculpture with sandblasted and engraved image with cut and polished finish, 16 cm in diameter.

3 Glass objects from the *Urban Life Series*, 2005 Blown glass sculpture with sandblasted and engraved image, 42–45 cm.

Inge Panneels

Space and light are the driving forces in Inge Panneels' work. Her studio, Idagos, produces an impressively diverse range of bespoke glass works, from domestically functional pieces through to architectural installations and open-air sculptures. The designs are bold, rich and vibrant, incorporating exciting textures into a contemporary aesthetic.

Since the majority of her works are site-specific and made to commission, Panneels' inspiration often comes from location and circumstance. Driven by a preoccupation with space and light, she considers glass as the most effective medium to explore such qualities:

Inspiration for my work is drawn from several sources (visual and literary) but a general theme is life's rich tapestry and universal mythology; providing me with strong concepts and images.

She communicates such inspiration using mostly kiln-based glass techniques, including casting, *pâte de verre*, fusing, slumping and enamelling. These glass elements are then often juxtaposed with other complementary materials such as stone, concrete, steel and timber.

In 2004, Panneels was commissioned to produce her most ambitious large-scale work, *Timekeepers*. Commemorating the recent excavations of two bodies from the Bronze and Iron Ages, the piece was composed of 42 separate multi-coloured glass panes spanning the entire two floors of a new social housing development.

Inge Panneels' studio, Idagos, is located in Scotland. Idagos' glass pieces have been commissioned by a variety of high profile clients including the NHS, Apex Hotels, Pizza Express and Lloyds TSB. As well as commissioned work, Panneels makes fine art sculptures that have been included in multiple exhibitions in Britain and her native country Belgium. These include Young Glass 2007 at the National Glass Centre and Hannah Peshar Sculpture Garden, Ockley. Panneels holds various workshops at Idagos Studios and lectures part-time at the University of Sunderland.

1

1 *Solid Hollow*, 2003
Cast iron, glass,
26 x 13 cm.
Photograph by I Gilmour.

2 Nest, 2005
Fused and *pâte
de verre* glass,
25 x 5 cm.
Photograph by I Gilmour.

3 *Nest (shallow)*, 2004
Cast glass with
pâte de verre rim,
25 x 5 cm.
Photograph by
Douglas Robertson.

3

Jeffery Sarmiento

Jeffery Sarmiento fuses text, pattern and image in his work, exploring ideas of place and ethnicity through intentional mismatches of symbolism and form. Born in Chicago, and educated at the University of Illinois and the Rhode Island School of Design, Sarmiento's work evidences a preoccupation with cultural metaphors and associations. Expressing his Filipino-American heritage through a self-referential displacement of various visual signifiers, the artist often chooses to overlay various visual elements to produce new meanings from iconic material. That is, Sarmiento re-arranges otherwise straight-forward visual elements in a play of cultural and aesthetic principles, encouraging the viewer to draw unlikely associations that open up the cultural play necessary to understand the work.

In his *Machete Wedding*, 2005, Sarmiento encases a grainy photograph in thick glass, etching various words and shapes on all six planes of the work. The photograph can only be viewed through the lens of the textual and figurative interventions Sarmiento employs, interrupting any transparent reading of the photographs. The tension between inherited and constructed cultural elements forms the basis for Sarmiento's work, which he chooses to present in the form of a glass book, extending the narrative elements he deploys elsewhere in his creative practice.

Though he now lives in Newcastle upon Tyne, Sarmiento continues to exhibit widely across America, with recent solo shows at the Robert Lehman Gallery in Brooklyn, New York, the Bullseye Connection Gallery in Portland Oregon and Solomon Fine Art in Seattle, Washington.

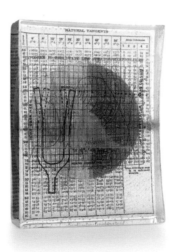

1

2

3

1,2&4 *Encyclopædia 1-8*, 2007
Enamelled and cast glass,
250 x 40 x 20 cm.

3 *Machete Wedding*, 2005
Enamelled and cast glass,
20 x 15 x 10 cm.
All photographs by
Kent Rogowski.

Jeffery Sarmiento

Ethan Stern

In Ethan Stern's work, surface interest and purity of form are juxtaposed, with texture, pattern and line overlaying his simple, abstract shapes. Evoking geographical imagery and textile design, his use of engraved line and pattern is graphic and painterly, suggesting both energy and movement.

American by birth, Stern studied ceramic art in Brisbane, Australia, and developed an interest in the vessel which led, on his return to America, to a move from the field of ceramics to glass. At Pilchuck Glass School in Stanwood, Washington, he began exploring the possibilities inherent in carved and engraved glass. The process opened doors for him, allowing him "to put together elements of colour, form, pattern and texture to create a unique voice within the material". By dulling the surface of the glass, he could redirect attention to such properties. Absorbing rather than reflecting light, the matt surfaces he produces echo both the richness and boldness of colour so often found in ceramics.

The transfer from the initial idea on paper to the object itself necessitates change, and for Stern this is part of a natural, organic process, as he develops the work spontaneously. "The evidence of the hand, the subtleties of surface and the creative process are vital the creation of my work", he claims.

Stern has taught glass-blowing and cold-working techniques with Hilltop Artists in Residence at Tacoma, Washington, The Appalachian Center for Craft in Tennessee, and Pratt Fine Arts Centre in Seattle, Washington. He is represented by the Chappell Gallery in New York, and the William Traver Gallery in Seattle. He owns and runs the Diamond Life Studio in Seattle.

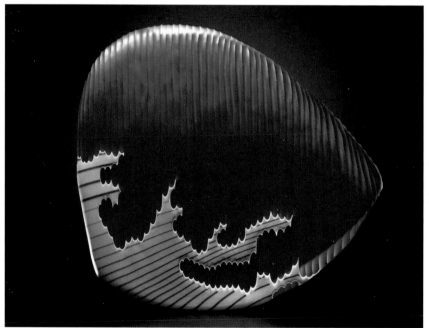

1

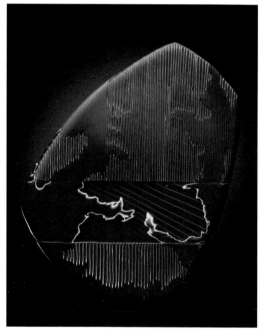

2

1 *Red Chew*, 2008
Blown and wheel
carved glass,
41 x 41 x 10 cm.

2 *Red Night*, 2008
Blown and wheel
carved glass,
43 x 38 x 8 cm.

3 *Hyde*, 2007
Blown and wheel
carved glass,
41 x 38 x 8 cm.

4 *White Hyde*, 2008
Blown and wheel
carved glass,
36 x 43 x 10 cm.

Sculpture

Anne Brodie

Anne Brodie's work draws upon her recent experiences of the changing natural world, which she witnessed first hand as part of a British Antarctic Survey team, supported by a Fellowship from the Arts Council in 2006–2007. Studying ice formations and patterns seems an appropriate activity for an artist with a background in glass sculpture. After originally training as a biologist, Brodie shifted her focus to art and graduated with an MA in glass from the Royal College of Art in 2003. Since then she has communicated a strong desire to free herself from materials in her practice, and to create the "least object objects" possible—inevitably leading to the incorporation of film and photography in her work. The temporality of such media readily serve to reinforce her attraction to transient materials, such as glass in its liquid state:

Hot, glowing, liquid glass is a seductive material with which to work, as is white porcelain slip, but I can't help but feel a little disappointed once they harden and become solid.

Brodie aims to reflect the malleability of the natural world, which is constantly moving and part of a cyclical process. She employs a thrift approach of incorporating into her work what ever she finds in her immediate environment—"dead insects, plastic bags and plaster". This focus on the minutiae of life is reflected in another of her ongoing projects funded by the Arts Council, involving Bioluminescence (natural light emissions from bacteria and algae) largely based on the scientific discoveries of microbiologist Dr Simon Park at Surrey University.

Brodie held the Arts Council Individual award two years running, 2004–2005, as well as winning the 2005–2006 Bombay Sapphire Prize for glass. In 2002 she accepted a scholarship from the Pilchuck Glass School and, in 2007, she was shortlisted for the Man Group Photography prize for work completed in Antarctica. She recently created a temporary installation based in the Silver and Sculpture Galleries at the Victoria and Albert Museum as part of the museum's 'Friday Late' series in conjunction with the exhibition Blood on Paper, 2008.

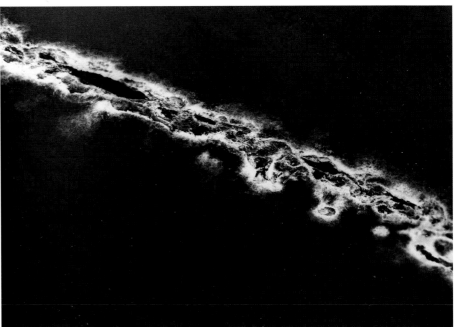

1

2

1 *Recycled Glass Threads and Sea Ice*, Antarctica, 2007 Temporary sculpture and photographic print.

2 *Glass Burn*, 2008 Hot glass and paper photographic print, 150 x 100 cm.

3 Temporary installation at the Victoria and Albert Museum Silver Galleries, 2008 Silver, silver cabinets and paper.

4 *Imposter*, 2007 Sculpture and Inkjet print.

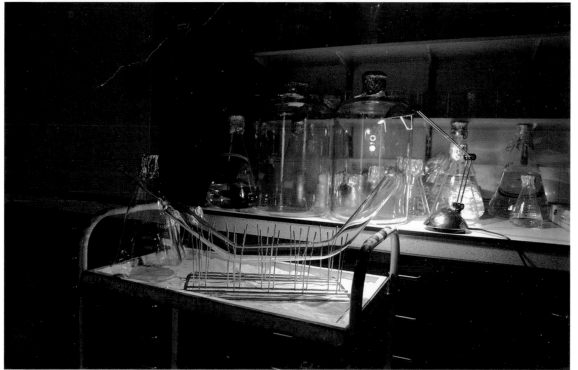

5

5 *Glass Hook*, 2005
Sculpture, glass and metal
and ivory button hook,
12 x 17 cm (one of
a series).

6 *Glass Stretch*, 2003
90 x 70 cm.

Anne Brodie

Stephanie Carlton Smith

Stephanie Carlton Smith claims to use glass for its ability to "define space and [to] express aspects of the human psyche". Recent works range from conventional glass objects such as bowls, vases and mirrors, to more sculptural forms—without a specific function—which have been shown in several galleries and exhibition spaces, including the Royal College of Art, Bedale Gallery, ArtParis, Turf, the London Art Fair, and Grosvenor House.

Carlton Smith combines a variety of traditional and contemporary techniques, such as slumping, bending, stretching and fusing in her practice. These delicate processes are labour intensive and, when employed, communicate something of the fallibility of hand-made creative processes. Carlton Smith has a strong sense of the psychic connection between her thought processes, and the object in hand, reflecting, to an extent, elements of existential philosophy: "It is our gaze that unites the individual fragments within the whole and in turn establishes the work's existence." And yet, her influences range widely from Persian literature to the poetry of Yeats—her sculpture *The Turning and Turning Gyre*, for example, is taken from the Yeats' poem *The Second Coming*, 1916.

The neat simplicity and minimalism of her sculptures to date, often made from clear glass and white porcelain, allows visual space for her intricate designs, which at times resemble scientific and biological structures such as DNA strands or chromosomes. The detail in her sculpture is central to her vision, as she explains:

The recurring imagery within my work has to be the containment of the fragmented interior, representing our fractured core and the beauty its complexity can present. Whether it be glass rods, slabs of plate, even groups of test tubes, they are gathered together and held in place by absolute structures.

Carlton Smith considers her work an extension of her own body—or rather the embodiment of her own thoughts and creativity, encased as they are in alabaster —a "symbolic and literal skin" holding the broken, cut glass in place.

1

2

1 *Mother*, 2007
  Borosilicate rod,
  alabaster,
  40 x 40 x 15 cm.

2 Ruby's Oval, 2007
  Borosilicate rod,
  jesmonite,
  38 x 28 x 10 cm.
  Photograph by
  Carlos Lumier.

3 *My Greek Swimming
  Pool*, 2006
  Low iron plate and
  plaster aggregate,
  38 x 28 x 10 cm.

Stephanie Carlton Smith

Annie Cattrell

Annie Cattrell's sculptures are a marriage of science and art; a culmination of ideas and technologies not usually associated with glass and which defy its material and conceptual boundaries. Rather than a body of work unified by a signature style or artistic aesthetic, Cattrell's glass sculptures have a shared spirit of curiosity. Their optical and physical qualities become a tool to reveal the invisible, to capture and expose everyday occurrences and the fleeting, intangible moments that are imperceptible to the naked eye.

Cattrell's practice is collaborative, and she treats glassmaking as an investigative rather than sculptural process. Borrowing the research and methodology of doctors, meteorologists, scientists, archaeologists and geologists, she challenges existing approaches to glassmaking, while subjecting the medium to medical, scientific and engineering processes.

Capacity, 2002–2007, one of her best-known works, is a series of anatomical sculptures that explore how medical technology can be applied to glass. Using Magnetic Resonance Imaging (MRI), she scans the interior of the human form, and translates the resultant image into three-dimensions. These sculptures—of lungs, the digestive and nervous system—show the invisible life of the human body and reveal a hidden view reserved only for doctors and surgeons:

It is the transformation and freezing into three-dimensions of iconographic subject matter that interests me: what happens when you contemplate something you think you know but shouldn't really be seeing this way. This three-dimensional vantage point allows the viewer to examine the subtle shifts and rhythms that ceaselessly occur in the natural world and within the body.

The intricacy and complexity of Cattrel's sculptures are realised by a similarly hybrid method. Instead of traditional glass-blowing or shaping techniques, her sculptures are formed using rapid prototyping technology, a laser engineering process usually employed to create three-dimensional models from computer data, to create precise and accurate sculpture.

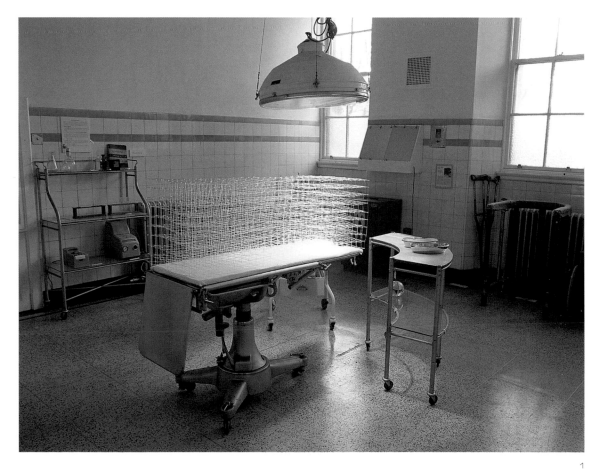

1

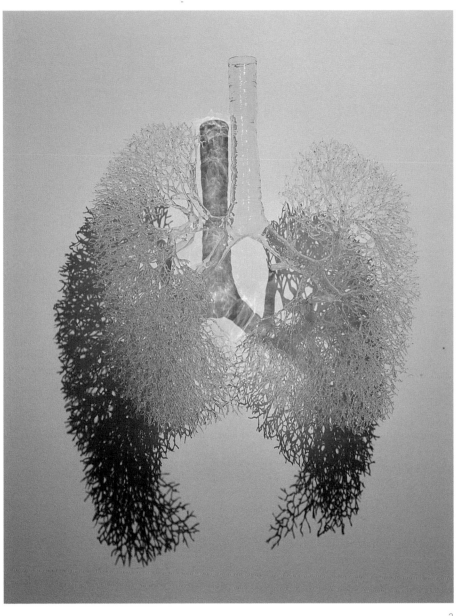

2

1 *Operating Theatre*, 2000   2 *Capacity*, 2000–2007
   Glass rod and operating   Glass lungs (edition
   table at the Crichton   of three),
   Hospital Museum, Dumfries   90 x 90 x 20 cm.
   Photograph by   Photograph by
   Allan Devlin.   Peter Cattrell.

3 *Conditions*, 2007
Sub-surfaced etched optical
glass (edition of three),
40 x 150 x 150 cm each.
Photograph by Peter Cattrell.

4 *Making Sense*, 2001
Glass rod and
furniture installation.

4

Dale Chilhuly

Dave Chihuly is one of the most prolific and influential American glass artists working today. His work ranges from environmental installations, to single vessels and multipart blown compositions.

Chihuly trained as an artist in the 1960s, a period that has greatly impacted upon his artistic output. A riotous, exploding use of colour, the blurring of the distinctions between art and craft, a movement away from the enclosed gallery space towards environments that are natural, open air and public and a collaborative approach to artmaking are all elements that define Chihuly's art and practice.

Chihuly first witnessed the collaborative approach to glass-blowing during his studies at the Venini factory in Venice. Since then, the teams he has amassed have worked to move the technique out of the confines of producing small, precious objects to realising large-scale, multi-part installations. As well as co-founding the Pilchuck Glass School in Washington, Chihuly has established several large studios in which artists work to develop the medium as a fine art.

Chihuly's blown compositions are 'mini environments' composed of freestanding organic structures. Over time he has built a unique vocabulary, using neon, argon and blown glass to combine intense colour with intricate line. 'Drawings' of pre-arranged glass threads are fused into the surfaces of vessels which are then blown in optic molds to create ribbed motifs. Over time the forms in his work have become elongated and linear, resulting in baroque, twisting, dynamic elements of churning colour and tone.

His architectural background has enabled him to create several outdoor installations in cities including Venice, Jerusalem and London. Such installations are built on a variety of surfaces, from pedestals to natural water to specially engineered structures. Chihuly's glass sculptures are included in more than 200 museum collections worldwide, including the Hokkaido Museum of Modern Art, the Metropolitan Museum of Art, the Museum of Modern Art, the Louvre, the Victoria and Albert and the Whitney.

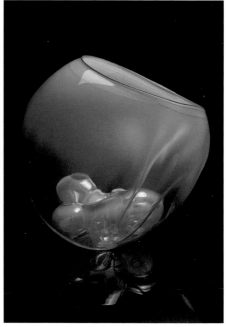

1

2

1 *Basket Grouping*, circa 1978

2 *Sky Blue Basket Set with Colbalt Lip Wraps*, 1992
43.2 x 38.1 x 40.6 cm.

3 *Persian Chandelier*, 2007
Phipps Conservatory
Pittsburgh, Pennsylvania.
All photographs by Terry Rishel.

3

5

4 *Persian Ceiling*, 2000
  Josyln Art Museum
  Omaha, Nebraska.

5 *Victoria and Albert Museum*
  Chandelier, 1999
  68.6 x 30.5 cm
  Victoria and Albert Museum
  London, England.
  All photographs
  by Terry Rishel.

Shirley Eccles

As an artist working in a variety of media, Shirley Eccles' approach to art is explorative, intuitive and distinguished by the challenges these media bring with them. Her multidisciplinary practice—including oil painting, ceramics, clay and glass—is testament to her interest in the, often unexpected, relationships that may be forged in the combination of techniques.

With the paradox of its utter solidity and fragility, and the sensuousness of its aesthetic qualities, glass has become a metaphor—in Eccles' work—for the ambiguities and inconsistencies of everyday life. Certain works demonstrate an interest in the passing of time and the intangible vestiges of human presence: a rope ladder with footprints in each frosted glass step, a glass slab swing with a relief impression of where someone may have sat. Here Eccles draws out the ethereal qualities of the medium through the representation of a possible past, glass becoming a material able to retain the traces of a brief interaction between body and object. The unspoken but innate kinetic energy of these works is uncannily juxtaposed with their absolute stillness, a factor given added emphasis through the play of light upon translucent glass and the vague, gossamer shadows it casts.

Eccles' practice is defined by her particular ability to blend the sculptural, aesthetic and technical in works by combining glass with other materials to form larger, unified artworks. Crucially, glass becomes (in this context) simply another appropriately and prudently chosen material, better able to exhibit its unique qualities.

Eccles extends her exploration of temporal subject matter in recent pieces, in which domestic objects are brought into curious and unique interactions with clear glass. A rusty ladle and antiquated kitchen colander hang from the wall, and replacing the liquid they might hold are 'pools' of glass, as though water petrified in motion. The briefest moment caught in time, these works are imbued with a particular nostalgia that gives the glass a narrative element and expressive positioning beyond the facts of its materiality.

Eccles' work explores the potential of glass' ability to express, as a sculptural material, not only its intricacies but also its symbolic and referential possibilities. In these pieces, glass carries complex properties in its ability to interrelate with other, seemingly incongruous materials, touching upon spheres beyond its physical and aesthetic values.

1

2

1 *Coagulation*, 2004
Glass and metal,
137 x 12 x 10 cm.

2 *Colander*, 2006
Glass and copper,
32 x 14 cm.
Photograph by
Gavin Wilkinson.

3 *Ladle* (detail), 2006
Glass and copper,
55 x 16 x 12 cm.
Photograph by
Gavin Wilkinson.

Beth Lipman

Beth Lipman creates still-lifes in hand-sculpted glass, paying homage to the paintings made by the seventeenth century masters of Germany, Spain and The Netherlands.

Still life paintings have conventionally been contemplated as aesthetically pleasing objects (with political, moral and theological undertones) that depict the temporality and beauty of nature and human existence; a tradition that Lipman harnesses to full effect. While such painting communicates controlled composition and the practice of technical skills, Lipman's glass works require a different type of precision—the ability to control the material at the moment of creation, through sculpting and blowing.

Bancketje, 2003, is arguably Lipman's most well-known piece—a three metre long glass banquet-style table complete with the remnants of a glass feast. Its intensive production process involved 15 glass-blowers (of varying skills), working together to create over four hundred glass tableware items to dress the installation. *Bancketje* metaphorically refers to the aftermath of each guest attending the event, depicting both the abundance of a feast, and its frivolity.

Working from painting, rather than an arrangement of objects, makes Lipman's still-lifes 'twice removed', the sculptural qualities of her glass pieces recreates the tangible third dimension of the original objects. The final manifestations of these works, however, are not the still-lifes themselves but the moment at which they are captured on film. Once recorded, the glass is destroyed or recycled. In so doing, Lipman returns the still-life to two-dimensions; the objects becoming as inaccessible and unattainable as the paintings that inspired them.

1

2

1 *Game Birds in a Niche (after Abraham Mignon)*, 2001
Glass and mixed media, 61 x 50.8 x 43.2 cm.

2 *Dead Birds (after Frans Cuyck van Myerop)*, 2002
Glass and mixed media, 91.4 x 76.2 x 20.3 cm.

3 *Bancketje*, 2003
Glass, mixed media, 213.3 x 609.6 x 127 cm.
All photographs by Eva Heyd.

4

4 *Cherries (after Sarah Miriam Peale)*, 2005
Mixed media,
30.5 x 25.4 x 12.7 cm.
Photograph by
Matthew Hollerbush.

5 *Fruit and Flower Centerpiece (II)*, 2007
53.3 x 30.5 cm.
Photograph by Jeff Machtig.

Andrew Paiko

Andrew Paiko's practice continually treads the line between function and abstraction, challenging preconceived notions of the roles that glass and sculpture perform. Paiko is interested in examining such questions metaphorically, making works that both speak of the relationships between nature, language and society and the challenges faced in everyday life, but which also have a perceived purpose.

The conflation of these concerns manifests itself in such works as *Seismograph*, 2006, a functional kinetic sculpture made from blown, sculpted and assembled glass that purports to read the various scales of earthquakes, and also in *Balance*, 2006, an intricately constructed set of measuring scales. Despite their perceived function,

however, these works are not high-tech, nor modern, the artist instead appropriating machines whose very antiquity would not see in them in use today.

Other works, such as *Canis Auribus Tenere*, 2007, (a glass vessel containing the skull of a coyote), and *Spine Jar*, 2008, (a coyote skull also housed in a vessel) are more macabre in tone and functionally ambiguous, hinting at an, almost obsessive preoccupation with death and preservation.

Paiko is evidently enthusiastic about the act of making and utilising specialist skills in his work, which is not only communicated in works like *Seismograph* and *Balance* but also through his continuing exploration of new methods of colouration,

form and pattern. He is preoccupied with the very materiality of glass, a form that is "pushed into space organically by a cumulative history of layering and motion". This notion of layering is one that is evident throughout the artist's practice through his collaging of fused cold glass and the complex details that adorn his sculptures.

Paiko co-founded the Central Coast Glass Artists' Studio, California, and has exhibited throughout North America, including exhibitions at The American Craft Council Retail Show, Baltimore, 2008, the Manette Gallery, Portland, 2007, the North Bank Gallery, Vancouver, 2007 and at Bergdorf Goodman, New York, 2006.

 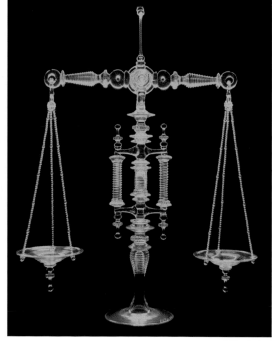

1

2

1 *Hourglass*, 2007
Blown, sculpted,
assembled glass, sand,
40 x 18 cm.

2 *Balance*, 2006
Functional kinetic
sculpture, blown,
sculpted,
assembled glass,
90 x 80 x 25 cm.

3 Seismograph, 2006
Functional kinetic
sculpture, blown,
sculpted, assembled
glass, motors, receipt
rolls, steel,
82 x 122 x 116 cm.

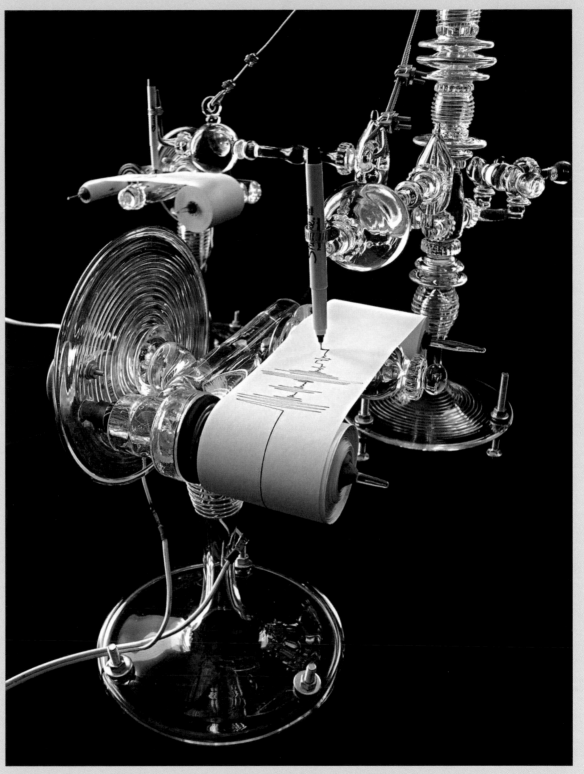

3

Angus M Powers

Currently teaching at the New York State College of Ceramics, Angus M Powers is a lecturer, teacher and practising glass artist, central to contemporary ceramics projects throughout America. Powers' work ranges from large-scale neon light installations, that comprise glass and steel structures, to small, often humorous, sculptures, such as his tiny parachuting figurines and repetitive use of tiny footprints on glass planetary solar system structures.

Works such as *Outdoor Light Semi*, draw inspiration from basic physical phenomenon, creating set pieces that resemble laboratory experiments. In these works, Powers is concerned with light, gravity, electricity, mass and atmosphere, and his work continually probes into the world of science, space and discovery.

Other works, like *Hundred Heads* for example (which displays a tray of identical miniature heads cast out of yellow glass), reveals Powers' fascination with ideas of cloning and reproduction, as well as a rejection of mass industrial processes.

Powers' work is darting, experimental and difficult to pin down to any one theory. He frequently changes style, method and concept, creating unique works that ultimately suggest the necessity for individual human touch in art.

Over the last few years Powers has been awarded a number of honours, including the Glass Art Society Emerging Artist Award, International Juried Competition, 2004. He was granted the Creative Glass Centre of America Fellowship in 2003, as well as receiving a second bursary from Contemporary Glass Philadelphia. In 2001 he was nominated for the Horizon Award, New York, at the New York Museum of Arts and Design as well as being selected for the Corning Scholarship Nomination, Seattle, at the Pilchuck Glass School in 2000.

1

1 *Incoming*, circa 1990s   2 *Hundred Heads*, circa 1990s

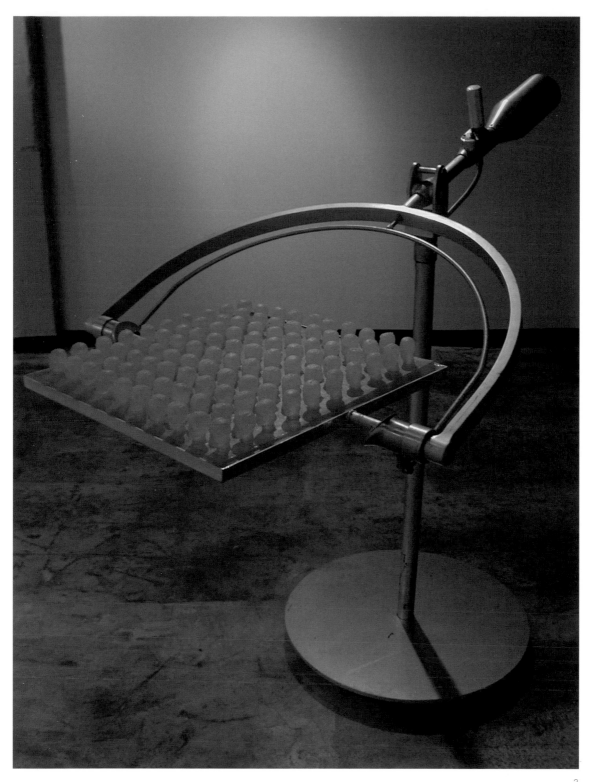

Minako Shirakura

Minako Shirakura is a Japanese artist living and working in America, whose practice is primarily concerned with the dichotomy of the medium of glass—encompassing both heat and cold, the fragile and the robust; it is precisely this reconciliation of opposites and contradictory qualities that reflect the way she perceives the world.

Shirakura's experiences outside her native country are of primary importance to her work, forever shaping her artistic practice. She explains:

My work includes a broad range of subjects and they often relate to my feelings and thoughts derived from [personal] experiences.... The experience of being outside of my own cultural sphere has given me the opportunity to view my surroundings from various perspectives. This helps me to see things I would have otherwise overlooked. The issues I deal with are personal on one level, but I believe that personal experience is often a doorway to a surprisingly universal subject.

Her installations using glass, mirrors, water and video projections are a masterful manipulation of light and shadow and create unsettling conditions for encountering the work. Our sense of gravity and space is inverted so that, instead of light shining onto Shirakura's installations, it seems to emanate from within them. The unique objects she builds such as *Thorn-Throne (in water)*, 2001, and the winter coat she constructed for the installation *Fur*, 2006, embody the smooth seduction of glass; made from a mass of glass filaments, they are at once inviting and foreboding.

Shirakura has received a BA (Hons) in glass, a Postgraduate Diploma from Edinburgh College of Art in Scotland and an MFA in Sculpture/Dimensional Studies from the New York State College of Ceramics at Alfred University. She has exhibited widely in Britain, Germany, Italy, Japan and America.

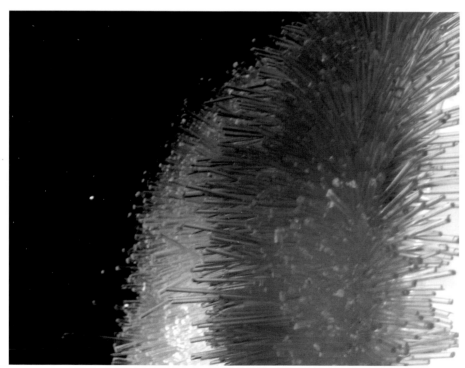

1

2

3

1&2 *Fur*, 2006
    Glass, metal,
    plastic sheet and
    video projection,
    119 cm in height.

3 *Before A Dream
    (detail)*, 2005
    Glass, wood, fishing
    wire and found objects,
    dimensions variable.

Hanna Stahle

For Hanna Stahle, glass is a provocative material, one that can be both reassuringly familiar and disturbingly foreign. Inspired by conceptual artists like William Kentridge and Jane Alexander, Swedish-born Stahle creates conceptual installations that pose controversial and open-ended questions.

Pleased, 2006, typifies Stahle's imagination at work. Here, a glass hand in a shiny silver glove reaches out, offering out luminous, otherworldly matter to the viewer. The familiar looking limb, combined with its strange glass offering, is both surreal and perturbing. "I try to give my artworks an atmosphere that is loaded with light", says Stahle.

The content is never intended to be unambiguous, and shall therefore hopefully give more than one association and interpretation. Gloves and hands are two symbols that constantly recur to me.

It interests me that they can represent [such] things as dissociation, care, responsibility, and power.

Pleased is disturbing not only for its interplay between the human and the unfamiliar, but also in its relationship to the architecture in which it is housed. Not only does it engage viewers, drawing them in with its semblance of human life, but it also seems to belong to the architecture—extending from the wall as though it were a continuation of the space, or evidence of a something else, behind the wall, trying to break out.

Stahle's interest in animating architectural surfaces is a recurrent theme. Just as she eschews a loyalty to a single material (working in ceramics, rubber, metal and video as well as glass) so too, she rebels against the white cube gallery format—by incorporating its existing architecture into her work.

Fosforus, the result of a collaboration with the artist, Mårten Medbo, also explores how the rigidity and flatness of gallery spaces can be ruptured. Here, using fluorescent glass and UV-light, a wall surface emits a faint phosphorescent glow, bearing light in the same way as the element after which it is named.

Trained as a sculptor, Stahle's work rejects the familiar rigidity and smoothness of glass. She cites the inability to completely control glass as that which drew her to the material—where chance is as much an influence as the skill of glass-blowers in the studio. Stahle is less concerned with creating perfect glass figures than she is with capturing the transformation between glass in its dynamic, liquid state, and its final, fixed form. She explores the organic qualities of glass, allowing it to succumb to natural elements, like centrifugal forces and gravity.

1

1 *Inside*, 2003
40 x 15 x 13 cm.

2&3 *Pleased*, 2006
Silverfoliated glass
and LED-light,
25 x 15 x 30 cm.

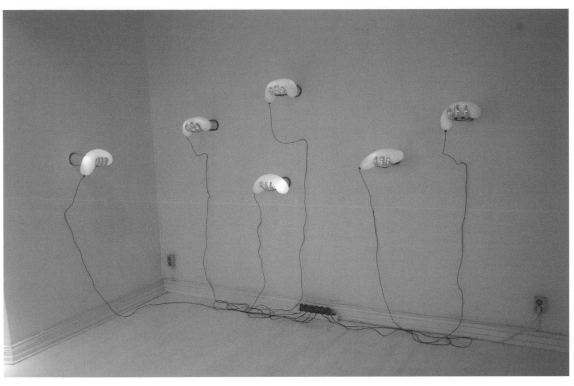

2

3

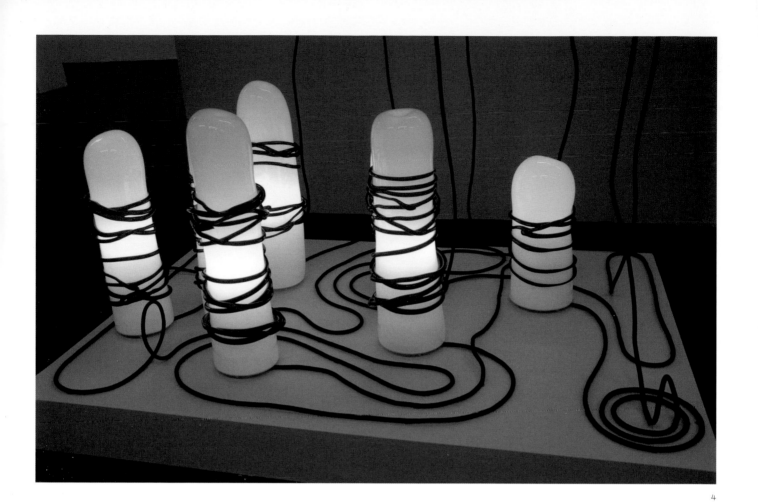

4

4 *Spools*, 2007
Glass, light and
rubber cable,
60 cm.

5 Hanna Stahle & Mårten Medbo
Fosforos, 2003
Vasseline glass, UV-light,
34 x 96 x 25 cm.

surface

Light

On Colour, Glass and Light

Heike Brachlow

It is obvious that colour as material and colour as light are extremely different; colour almost always seems applied, except for raw materials and they are seldom bright.[1]

Glass could be seen as a material that allows colour to take form, a material that merges colour, form and light. However, discussion of colour is difficult, colour vocabulary scarce and not always understood. Even the most basic terms are interpreted subjectively. In Part I of his *Interaction of Color*, Joseph Albers begins: "If one says 'red' (the name of a colour) and there are 50 people listening, it can be expected that there will be 50 reds in their minds. And one can be sure that all these reds will be very different."[2] Clearly, even a simple discussion of colour poses difficulties. How, then, does one discuss colour in glass, with its many different modes of appearance and its many contributing factors? As minimalist artist, Donald Judd, suggests:

> After a few decades the discussion of colour is so unknown that it would have to begin with a spot. How large is it? Is it on a flat surface? How large is that? What colour is that? What colour is the spot? Red. If a second spot is placed on the surface, what colour is it? Black? What if both spots were red, or black? How far away is the black spot from the red spot? Enough for these to be two discrete spots, one red and one black? Or near enough for there to be a pair of spots, red and black? Or apart enough for this to be uncertain? What if the red and black spots are next to each other? And of course, which red?[3]

A discussion on colour in glass would have to begin with a simple three-dimensional form, for example, a cuboid: How large is it? Is it transparent or opaque? Are there variations in thickness? What about the surface? Is it textured? Polished? Matt? What colour is it? Where does the illumination come from? How strong is it? What type is it? How does the colour change when the type of illumination changes? What happens if the direction of illumination changes?

Presumably, Albers' and Judd's reds are opaque; the colour of a surface, which is the appearance of colour discussed in the majority of literature. Other types of colour—transparent colours—are (if at all) mentioned briefly, with differing definitions. For articulation of modes of appearance of colour, psychology, physiology (studies in perception) and physics offer some possibilities; although artists empirically engage with colour, they do not often articulate their findings.

One of the biggest differences between glass and most other materials is its transparency. Colour can be opaque or simply located on an object's surface. This film can work to obscure a work's interior or, where it thins out, reveal glimpses of the same such area (as can be found in many of Dale Chihuly's sculptures, for example).

How can these different modes of colour be described? The two most common terms used for transparent colour that are not surface colour are 'volume colour' and 'film colour'. Albers explains volume colour using the example of a coloured liquid: "Tea in a spoon will appear lighter than tea in a cup; the blue of a swimming pool will appear darker in deeper water." Gestalt psychologist David Katz describes volume colour as "colours which are seen as organised in and filling a tri-dimensional space" (however, for him the true property of volume colour is expressed only when these colours are genuinely transparent).[4]

Film colour, according to Albers, appears as a thin, translucent layer between the eye and an object. Katz describes it as the colour experience one has when looking through "a piece of smoked glass of medium transparency or a piece of coloured gelatine, held at arm's length in such a way that its boundaries are visible".[5] The *Coleman Dictionary of Psychology* defines it as "a misty appearance of colour without any fixed distance that is experienced when there are no lines or edges present in the visual field".[6]

I understand 'film colour' as the colour of light or air, an appearance of colour without a definite location or boundary. 'Volume colour' is that of a transparent solid whose mass appears to have tonal qualities. For the purpose of this text, I will use the term 'colour film' to describe a thin transparent coloured layer.

The other major considerations in the discussion of colour and glass are surface quality and form—the surface can be matt or glossy, textured or smooth; each of these properties will impact differently on the way light is transmitted, reflected, refracted, diffused, and scattered. Form, of course, has a huge impact on the appearance of colour—and vice versa.

Transmitted Light and Coloured Shadows

When thinking of colour, light, and glass, stained glass comes to mind. The practice of modifying light in great buildings is an age-old technique: from thin alabaster slabs in ancient Egypt to horn and oiled linen in the Middle Ages, window coverings were used to mute the bright sunlight, and modify the atmosphere inside. There is some evidence of stained glass having been used for windows as early as in Byzantine times. Certainly, by the Middle Ages, stained glass was a well-developed art, used especially in buildings that require an atmosphere of reverence—Christian churches. Colour became important for its symbolic as well as decorative and light-transforming properties, as stained glass church windows were used widely to disseminate the scriptures to the masses. The interiors of churches were transformed by light, coloured shadows logging the passage of the day, the path of the sun, changes in the weather, the passing of seasons, and continually changing.

Today, although church communities continue to commission stained glass, increasingly, architectural glass is made for secular buildings like shopping centres, train stations and corporate buildings. Coloured glass is not only used for windows but also for additional illumination, as in a recent work of Udo Zembok in the Crypt of Chartres Cathedral. The concept of stained glass windows is used for the dual purposes of art and lighting: In the Crypt, a 'light wall', a monumental coloured glass wall, gently illuminates its surroundings, its turquoise colour reminiscent of the water of baptism. However, through its unchanging nature, artificial illumination completely changes the character of the glass: the colour remains consistent.

Colour Membranes—Transparent, Translucent and Opaque

Glass art comes from a long-standing tradition of vessel making. Initially small, opaque and core-formed, by the fifth century BC, techniques of casting and cutting were employed to make larger, more sophisticated vessels. Due to time-consuming manufacturing techniques, glass objects remained luxury articles until the first century BC, when they were established in Rome and at other Italian sites. From then on, vessels became more varied in form and function, more affordable and often brightly coloured. At this time, the predominant technique employed. Casting was slowly supplanted by glass-blowing in the first century AD. The speed and ease of production that could be achieved by employing

Opposite:
Stained glass window
depicting St Catherine
from Partenheim,
circa 1440
Image courtesy of
Hessisches Landesmuseum,
Darmstadt, Germany/The
Bridgeman Art Library.

Top:
Udo Zembok
*Rideau de Lumière
(Curtain of Light)*, 2006
Fused float glass,
inclusions of pigments,
460 x 280 x 0.2 cm.
Image courtesy of
the artist.

Bottom:
Lino Tagliapietra
Endeavour, 2004
Blown and battuto cut
glass, steel cable,
dimensions variable.
Collection of The Corning
Museum of Glass,
Corning, New York.

the latter technique allowed glassware to become ubiquitous as functional items, aided by the invention of mould blowing in approximately AD 25.

Taking into account this history, the emphasis on functionality in glass manufacture and the fact that many studio glass artists came from a background in ceramics (where the container is a core shape), it is not surprising that, from the beginning, the vessel form was universally employed and explored in the studio glass movement.

Artist and teacher, Lino Tagliapietra, is a master in traditional Venetian techniques. His elegant vessels display intricate patterns, juxtapositions of transparent and opaque glass and subtle surface treatment. Tagliapietra uses pattern and colour to accentuate form and achieve optical effects, and frequently employs traditional techniques of lathe-cutting to attain velvety textured surfaces that diffuse the light.

Venetian glass has influenced many studio artists, the most noted student of which is Dale Chihuly, whose combination of the American style and Venetian techniques has been championed by many. With the help of a team of master glass-makers, he makes brightly-coloured organic shapes which are assembled into large installations. A gifted colourist, he employs a bright, contrasting palette. Chihuly has always taken a painterly approach to glass, as evidenced by such work as *Irish Cylinders*, 1975, in which he used glass vessels as a canvas for figurative drawing. Over time Chihuly's drawings became looser and less figurative, and colour more important.

Chihuly's pieces employ a mixture of opaque and transparent colours. However, his vessels are thin-walled and there appears to be no mass behind their surface colours, only empty volume. Often, some or all of the outside colours and patterns are visible on the inside. Or, as many of his *Basket Set* series demonstrate, opacity gradually becomes translucent, allowing an obscured view of the objects inside.

Illusions in Optical Glass

In the 1660s, Isaac Newton discovered that a prism, traditionally made of clear glass, could split light into a spectrum of colours when struck by a narrow beam of sunlight.[7] Although translucency is generally thought to be the 'natural' appearance of glass, this is not actually true. Clear glass is more difficult to achieve than many coloured glasses became sand, which makes up the bulk of the glassmaking raw material, always contains impurities—usually in form of iron oxide, which lends a greenish/brownish tint. To counteract this, other oxides, for example manganese or cerium oxide, are added as decolourisers. One of the major goals of glass-makers from the fifteenth century onward has been to achieve a perfectly clear glass: a difficult task. Even today, companies such as Steuben, for example, undertake the painstaking process of examining every block of lead crystal separately for bubbles.

Glass artists extensively play with the optical properties of glass in their work. American artist John Kuhn, for instance, creates glass objects that make use of mirror effects, refraction and reflection. They are cut, polished and assembled from many precisely cut pieces of mostly clear glass, revealing an infinity of shapes and colours. The optical properties of the glass, together with light, result in constant movement and change.

British artist, Colin Reid, polishes the surfaces of his monumental works to achieve transparency, creating windows to the interior of the work, and to effect illusions caused by refraction. As one walks around the work, surfaces change from transparent to mirror-like while, at certain angles, the textured motif appears larger, at others smaller.

Due to the Bohemian tradition of glass cutting and polishing in the Czech Republic, many glass artists work with the properties of polished glass, often in a subtle and ambiguous ways, as demonstrated by Vaclav Cigler's sculptures in the Corning Museum of Glass. Optical sculptures, however, are not necessarily clear: they can be any colour. This is amply demonstrated in the prism-like coloured wedges of Pavel Trnka, which clearly show properties of volume colour—a wide, intensely coloured block tapers into a clear thin edge, to nothingness. Sitting next to, or partly behind, another wedge, of another colour, they reflect, refract, and confuse. No luminous glow here, only reflections, sharp edges and bent light, mirroring and illusion.

Volume Colour

Volume colour fills three-dimensional space and changes appearance with different thicknesses. An illusion of volume colour can be achieved through optical effects. If a clear sculpture is assembled by lamination of cut and polished parts, the glue lines act from certain angles as reflectors, while being completely invisible from other angles. If the glue is tinted the whole object can appear coloured from some angles. From other angles, it will be clear.

In his essay "Some Aspects of Color in General and Red and Black in Particular" minimalist artist, Donald Judd, observes that "colour to continue had to occur in space", exploring colour with an almost mathematical precision in his three-dimensional work. Glass artists are able to take the concept one step further: what better way for colour to 'occur in space' than in a transparent solid? Coloured pieces of solid glass are mostly cast, and one of the earliest known examples is a small portrait of an Egyptian King from 1450–1400 BC, held in the collection of the Corning Museum of Glass. It is made from blue glass but, due to a long burial, it is now coated with a tan substance, which makes it appear opaque.

Transparent volume colour can be observed in cast monochrome cups, bowls and vases from Assyria, dating between 725—600 BC. A well-known example is the Sargon Vase in the British Museum. Here, the surface is matt and there are variations from thick to thin, with obvious colour changes.

Volume colour made another appearance in the first century AD, with Roman monochrome cast vessels. These are similar to Hellenistic ribbed bowls from the fifth century BC, but unlike their predecessors, employ colour, rather than being clear. Mostly blue or purple, they show a thick-thin colour change due to the ribbing.[8]

Today, the glass casting centre is the Czech Republic. There, from behind the iron curtain, casting developed independently from the Western studio glass movement. Building on a tradition of factory glass, Czech artists, led by husband and wife team Stanislav Libenský and Jaroslava Brychtová, developed new casting and annealing techniques, and for the first time it became possible to cast large solid glass forms. While glass artists were working mostly with vessels elsewhere, here a tradition of fully-fledged sculpture and large-scale architectural work was established. Libenský and Brychtová collaborated over a period of 48 years, producing a large body of work that demonstrates a thorough exploration of light and colour in space. They began experimenting with volume colour, or 'painting with light', in the late 1950s and early 60s in relief works such as *Animal Reliefs*, *Lap* and *Grey Composition*. From thin, light areas to dark thick areas, a whole palette of monochromes is available to 'paint' with. Three-dimensional curves and angles translate into subtle shading of light and dark.

Top:
Lino Tagliapietra
Hopi, 1996
Blown with filigree cane,
69.2 cm.
Collection of The Corning
Museum of Glass, Corning,
New York.

Bottom:
*Portrait of King Amenhotep
II, Egypt*, BC 1436-1411
Deep blue glass.
Collection of The Corning
Museum of Glass, Corning,
New York.

Opposite:
Dale Chihuly
*Benaroya Hall Silver
Chandelier*, 1998
Photograph by
Theresa Batty.

Libenský and Brychtová's exploration into clear optical glass and the way it interacts with light began in the 1970s, with the initial small-scale sculpture *Sphere in Cube*, 1970, quickly leading to large-scale architectural work.

Their knowledge of volume colour and optical geometric sculpture was combined in the 1980s, most notably in their *Head* series. In these pieces, geometric shapes are divided by angular planes, and polished surfaces both reflect and refract the light, while matt, translucent surfaces contain the light and obscure views into the interior. The full beauty of these pieces is only revealed with time: as the ambient light changes, so does the light within. Different panes light up and turn dark; and again, one has to turn to optics to try and understand these phenomena.

The glass used in Libenský and Brychtová's castings is usually monochrome, although often, a single casting appears to have several colours. *Red Pyramid*, for example, presents not only a change in colour value (lightness) as the volume changes from thick to thin, it actually shows a change in hue: from yellow to red to brown. *Green Eye of the Pyramid* changes from deep green to a bright greenish-yellow. Much of Libenský and Brychtová's knowledge of colour and light comes from empirical explorations. In *Green Eye of the Pyramid*, for example (which consists of two intersecting parts of a half cone) the eye glows as if lit from behind: the artists themselves were surprised by this effect. [9]

Clear or White?

A Captive Audience, a piece in the contemporary glass collection in the Victoria and Albert Museum by David Reekie, is made from clear glass. However, it doesn't appear clear, but rather translucent white, and impossible to see through. Such an effect is caused by its matt surface, which scatters, diffuses and internally reflects the light and causes a whitish translucence and luminous glow from within. If these pieces where polished, like Koichiri Yamamoto's vessel parodies, they would appear transparent.

Reekie's new body of work, *Exchange of Information*, contains both surface colour, in form of enamels applied in a painterly fashion on the bases, and translucent volume colour in the heads. These have a slightly soapy, alabaster-like appearance, which is characteristic of the *pâte de verre* technique of casting, resulting from the glass being suffused by small bubbles that internally diffuse and reflect light. The luminosity of Reekie's heads gives a transient appearance, emphasised by the contrast with the opaque, solid, surface-coloured bases.

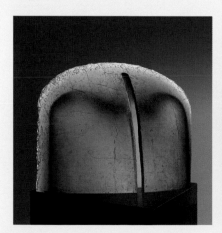 

Left:
Stanislav Libenský and
Jaroslava Brychtová
*Imprint of an Angel
II*, 1999
Mold-melted glass, steel
pedestal; cut, ground,
polished,
77.5 cm.
Collection of The Corning
Museum of Glass, Corning,
New York.

Right:
Stanislav Libenský and
Jaroslava Brychtová
Red Flower, 1976
Mold-melted glass;
aluminium base,
120 cm.
Collection of The Corning
Museum of Glass, Corning,
New York.

Pâte de verre refers to the sintering or melting of granules of glass in a mould, which creates a semi-opaque to translucent appearance. This can be done by either applying a paste of glass powder and a binder to the surface of a mould (for thin-walled pieces), or by filling the whole mould with glass granulates. Varying degrees of translucency can be achieved by controlling the temperature and length of the firing. The glass can be grainy and opaque if only just sintered (as in Diana Hobson's delicate vessels) or translucent (Argy-Rousseau's 1885–1953 figures and Steven Easton's *The Snow Queen's Realm*, 2004–2005, are two such examples). Developed in the second half of the nineteenth century by sculptor Henry Cros, 1840–1907, the technique was extensively used in the late nineteenth and early twentieth centuries. As other cast glass solids, *pâte de verre* objects exhibit distinct luminosity from within. However, because of the countless bubbles, the quality of luminosity is different.

Opalescent Glass

The term opalescent describes a translucent milky appearance similar to *pâte de verre*. However, the effect results from colouring agents in, or treatment of the glass, rather than the particle size before casting, and this glass is usually bubble-free. Opalescent glass was developed during the Art Nouveau period and extensively used by Louis Comfort Tiffany and René Lalique. Usually seen in pressed or mould-blown glass, a colour change can often be observed between thick and thin areas of the glass—milky white, for example, often changes to blue in thick areas. Opalescent pressed glass can look similar to *pâte de verre*, and also appears to glow from within.

Contrary to other materials, in glass it is possible to have a complete absence of colour. The optical properties of clear transparent glass have been utilised by many artists. Clear glass is the material of choice for a variety of reasons: Reekie uses it to create neutral generic figures, while in Silvia Levenson's work, it can lend a sense of unreality or absence. Her pieces include children's shoes and clothes, their pastels reminiscent of the colouring in old photos, or translucent knifes raining down on a candy-coloured village. Beth Lipman's blown still-life sculptures recreate old paintings, and absence of colour expresses opulence and old-world charm, using the idea of a disdain for colour as a mark of refinement and distinction, as it used to be seen in several European and Oriental cultures.

Colour in glass can appear as volume or surface colour, as a transparent membrane or as a solid coloured mass, as spectral colours and optical illusions. However, its appearance always depends on the illumination. Physicists say that colour is light, and since I have started working with rare earth glasses, I am inclined to agree. Rare earth elements,

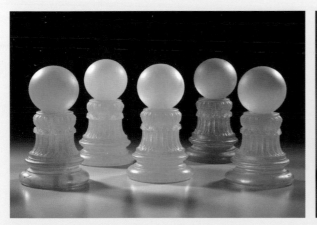
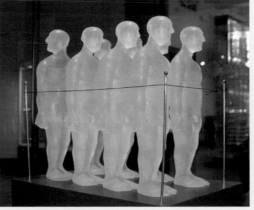

especially neodymium oxide, used as colouring agents in glass, cause colour to change in different lighting conditions. An object that is pink in daylight, for example, can be bright green in fluorescent light, yellow in led light, and blue in sodium mercury high intensity discharge (HID) lamps. Suddenly, the colour doesn't belong to the object any more, it is a separate factor, and changeable in a way that can't be overlooked. This, for me, exposes and shifts all sorts of preconceptions. Glass, therefore, is no longer a medium whose 'objecthood' can be readily fixed or categorised.

1   Judd, Donald, *Complete Writings 1959–1975*, New York: New York University, p. 200.
2   Albers, Josef, *Interaction of Colour*, New Haven and London: Yale University Press, 2006.
3   Judd, Donald, "Some Aspects of Colour in General and Red and Black in Particular", *ArtForum*, Summer, 1994.
4   Katz, David, *The World of Colour*, London: Kegan Paul, Trench, Trubner & Co. Ltd, 1935.
5   Katz, *The World of Colour*, p. 17.
6   Coleman, AM, *A Dictionary of Psychology*, Oxford University Press, 2001.
7   See: http://en.wikipedia.org/wiki/Isaac_Newton
8   Price, Richard W, *The Corning Museum of Glass: A Guide to the Collections*, Corning, New York: The Corning Museum of Glass, 2001.
9   Kehlmann, Robert, *The Inner Light, Sculpture by Stanislav Libenský and Jaroslava Brychtová*, Seattle: The Museum of Glass, 2002, p. 33.

Top:
René Lalique
Victoire, The Spirit of the Wind (date unknown)
Frosted and clear glass car mascot, with pale amethyst tint.
Private Collection/©
Dreweatt Neate Fine Art Auctioneers, Newbury, Berks, Britain/The Bridgeman Art Library, ADAGP, Paris and DACS, London 2008.

Bottom:
Martin Rosol
Blue Eye, circa 2000
Image courtesy the artist and PRISM Contemporary Glass.

Brian and Jenny Blanthorn

Husband and wife duo Brian and Jenny Blanthorn have worked together on their glass sculptural and functional pieces since 1983, creating their trademark striated and iridescent works using a number of techniques, processes and custom designed machinery perfected over the 30 years of working together.

Inspired by the naturally occurring patterns of oceanic and mountain rock formations and the vibrant colours found in tropical marine life, the globular, pebble sculptures harbour a myriad of optical illusions, visual interferences and subtle colour variations that alter the viewers' vantage-point; seeming from one perspective merely naturally occurring rock or crystal boulders but from another, as if made of some gaseous extra-terrestrial material.

The highly time-consuming and technically complex production process that goes into each piece arises from the synthesis of the couple's individual interests and areas of technical expertise; Brian's interests in ceramics and the construction of glass-working machinery and Jenny's background in textiles and pattern-making. Layers of flat sheet glass are painted or block printed using sponging and dragging techniques—creating a galaxy of colours and subtle pattern variations in the finished work—before being assembled in the kiln in complex multiple laminate arrangements. After firing at between 800 and 950 degrees centigrade, the pieces undergo the chiselling, grinding, polishing and waxing stages that determine their finished forms; each piece taking as long as two to three months to complete.

Using either combinations of clear and dichroic glass which, due to its thin layer of minerals and metals, gives the chromatic internal reflections of pieces such as W278, 2005, or dichroic and 'opalescent' glass which generates the highly colourised and holographic effect of pieces such as W283, 2006, the volatility of kiln-formed compounds of flat sheet glass and subtle variations in the multi-staged fabrication process guarantees each piece its own uniqueness while maintaining the distinctive stamp of the Blanthorn's highly skilled and painstaking practice.

As well as their sculptural pieces, Brian and Jenny Blanthorn have worked on architectural commissions throughout England and have exhibited in a number of galleries and art fairs in London and New York.

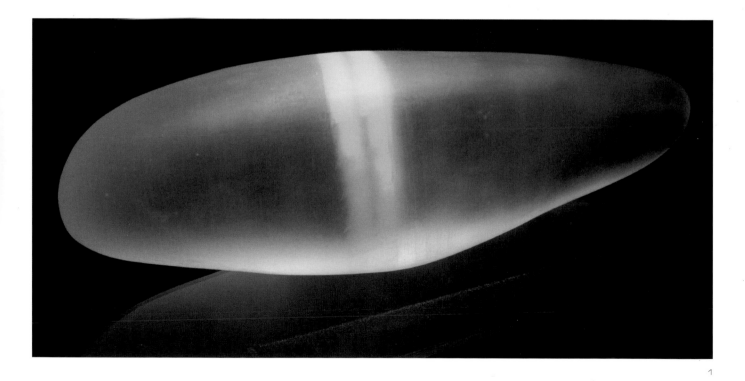

1

1 *Large boulder optical type glass and Dichroic glass, 2005 33 x 50 x 9 cm.*

2 *Optical type glass and Dichroic glass, 2008 53 x 19 x 8 cm.*

3 *Large boulder 'opalescent' glass and Dichroic glass, 2006 50 x 29 x 8 cm.*

2

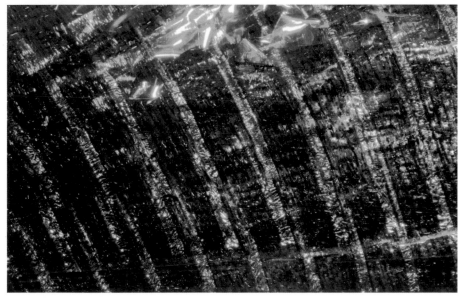

3

Brian and Jenny Blanthorn

Bocci

Bocci is an architecture and design practice based in Vancouver, Canada, specialising in limited edition, custom-made fabrications and installations. Bocci's work is a precious alternative to the prefabricated, standardised and mass-produced products now flooding the contemporary market.

Bocci's stunning lighting pieces explore the medium of the chandelier within a contemporary design landscape. Their first product, the 14 *Series*, consists of low voltage pendant lights designed to hang in clusters. Each pendant is a hand crafted seamed cast glass sphere with a frosted cylindrical void, inside of which is housed a ten watt halogen light. The pendants radiate a subtle glow as the light emitted interacts with the imperfections of the cast glass—when multiplied they gain in strength to give the effect of candles floating in frozen water. Bocci's luminary installations are limitless in size and scope and can accumulate in power according to the client's desires. They are currently developing a series of CSA and UL approved electrical accessories as a further step in their mission to revolutionise the aesthetics of interior design.

Bocci's creative director, Omer Arbel, was architecturally trained in the 1990s, a background that now informs the company's creative output. Arbel's design received great popular acclaim with the highly sculptural 2.4 chair in 2003. 2.4 was the recipient of numerous awards including a Chicago Atheneaum Good Design Award, ID magazine honorable mention, and D&AD Yellow Pencil shortlist. 2.4 is now housed in the permanent collection of the Chicago Atheneaum Museum of Architecture and Design, while *Wallpaper Magazine* recently selected Arbel as one of 15 up-and-coming contemporary designers.

1

1 Omer Arbel
14 Series Light, 2007

2 Omer Arbel
21 Series
Chandelier, 2007
White porcelain
and frosted blown
Pyrex glass.

Lisa Cahill

Lisa Cahill is an Australian artist who creates minimalist-inspired, abstract glass wall panels that draw inspiration from her own personal experiences of the vibrant colours, textures and space of the Australian outback and the bleak winter landscape of her native Denmark. Using two to six panels per work, the structural line of the rectangular glass panelling is echoed in her muted, linear etches and hint at the urban built environment—telephone masts or the outline of distant buildings. In works such as *Frozen Memories*, 2005, and *Distant Memories*, 2005, the line between the built and natural environment is constantly suspended by the slightness of the figuration; as urban *leitmotifs* evaporate into ghostly vistas. Other, more abstract, works play upon the associations of composition and colour and gesture toward elemental forces such as light and weather conditions. Influenced by elements of traditions such as colour field and minimalism Cahill's seemingly familiar, yet abstract, landscapes document her own personal recollections while also prompting similar meditative responses from the viewer.

Using a variety of refined techniques to create her kiln-formed glass panels as well as her smaller functional pieces, Cahill's practice mirrors the economy of the visual result. Using layers of both transparent and opaque glass, the artist carves onto or through the surface using a diamond lathe wheel to create varying degrees of texture and depth as well as using methods such as sandblasting and etching to reveal intensities of underlying colour.

Establishing her own kiln-forming studio in 2002, Cahill has co-ordinated workshops and lectured on kiln forming throughout Australia as well as exhibiting widely across that country, America and China.

1

1 *The Old Man and The Sea*, 2002
Kiln-formed and engraved glass,
42 x 94 x 0.7 cm.
Photograph by David McArthur.

2 *Unveiling Light*, 2006
Kiln-formed and wheel carved glass panels,
(set of three),
89 x 50 x 0.6 cm.
Photograph by Greg Piper.

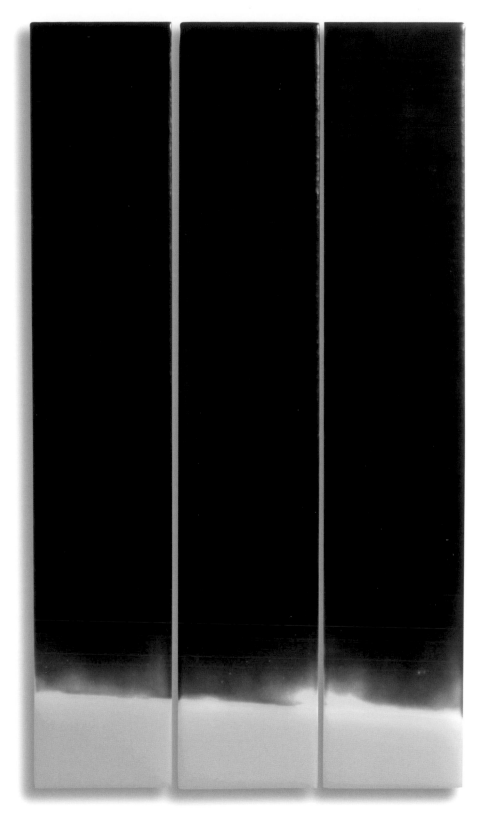

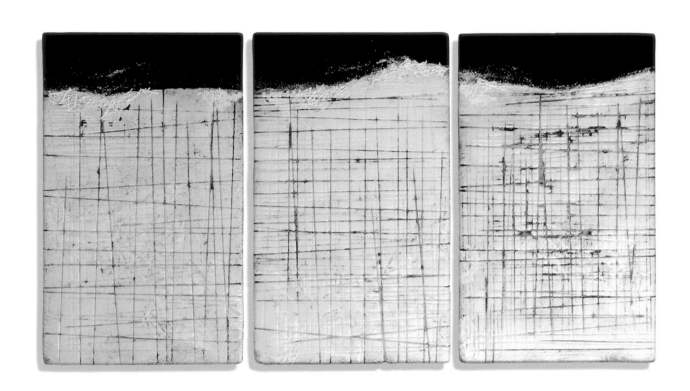

4

3 *Tempest #2* (detail), 2007
  Kiln-formed and
  carved glass panels
  (set of three),
  63 x 106 x 0.8 cm.
  Photograph by Greg Piper.

4 *Behind the Lines*, 2003
  Kiln-formed carved
  and glass panels
  (set of three),
  49.5 x 95 x 0.7 cm.
  Photograph by Rohan Young.

Olafur Eliasson

Appealing to all the senses, Danish-Icelandic artist Olafur Eliasson's sculpture and installation work draws attention to the natural and material worlds that surround us. Visually seductive and playful, his work belies mechanical science at work. Describing his work as a "machine" or "phenomenon maker", he invites human interaction in his practice.

Based in Berlin and operating out of Studio Olafur Eliasson, an experimental laboratory for spatial research, his projects range from small-scale sculptural mediations to architectural collaborations such as the 2007 Serpentine Pavilion which he conceived of, and developed with, Norwegian architect Kjetil Thorsen.

His works have simulated other aspects of the weather and natural phenomena—in for *Your Windless Arrangement*, 1997, for example, the artist installed 14 ventilators to channel a stream of wind through the Malmö Art Museum in Sweden. Using a simple pipe and pump mechanism elevated on a tower of scaffolding, *Waterfall*, 1998, introduced the commotion of tumbling water into a museum atrium in Madrid, Spain. In each situation the audience is at once confronted with a sensuous experience while also being made aware of the relatively inexpressive technology at work behind it.

Eliasson's work in glass is awe-inspiring and seemingly beyond the realms of materiality. Installations such as *Spectral Projection*, 2005, and *Halo Window*, 2005, employ acrylic and hologram glass and projection lamps to create unexpected spatial effects with refracted light and shadow. *Sunset Kaleidoscope*, also from 2005, comprises a motorised kalidescopic box installed into an existing window frame. Mirrored images of the gallery interior are spliced with the distorted view outside and a repeating reflection of a rotating yellow disc.

Eliasson's work features in high profile public and private collections across the globe. He has had solo shows at the Solomon R Guggenheim Museum, New York, The Museum of Contemporary Art, Los Angeles and the Deste Foundation, Athens. *The Weather Project* was his landmark commission for the Turbine Hall at Tate Modern, London in 2004.

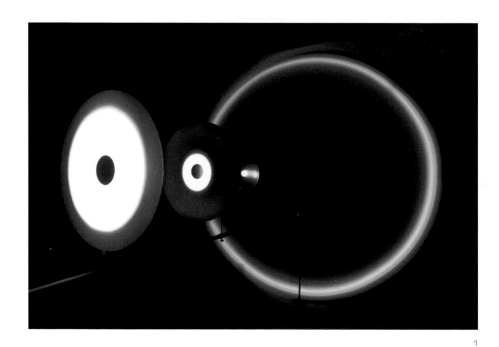

1

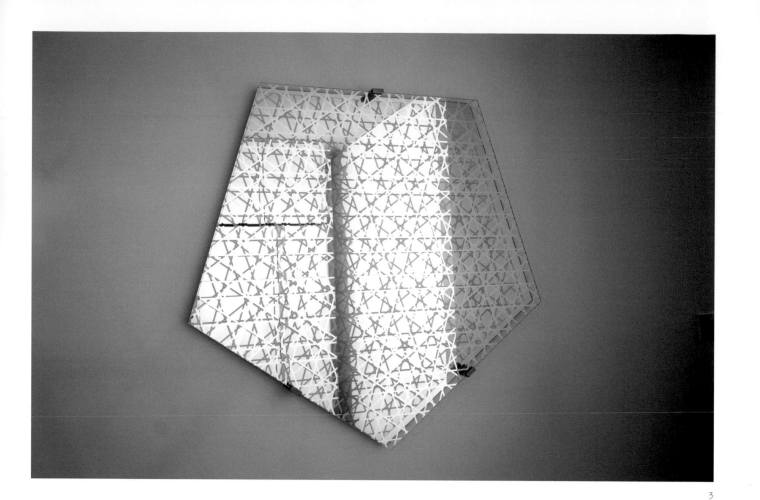

3 *Garden Mirror*, 2004
Glass, mirror and stainless
steel, halogen lamp,
120 x 124.5 x 9 cm.

4

4 *Sunset Kaleidoscope*, 2005
Wood, mirror, acrylic
glass and motor,
35.5 x 35.5 x 193 cm.
All images courtesy of
West of Rome Inc, Los Angeles.
All photographs by
Fredrik Nilsen.

Anne Gant

American artist, Anne Gant, uses hot glass as a tool to create her delicate and ambiguous prints and drawings. First, she sculpts the hot glass into shapes with carefully etched patterns, which she then presses against wet sheets of rag paper, "while the glass is still screaming hot from the glory hole". This evocative process leaves smoking, burning impressions on the paper, producing mysterious "maps of that heat", which are reminiscent of the explosive gunpowder installations of artist, Cai Guo Quiang, in their unpredictability and seeming lack of control.

The theory implicit in Gant's work has its roots in abstract romanticism; hinting at the idea of a "secret aspect of the glass... normally known only to the maker". The marks she makes form a mysterious language, which she hopes can be tapped into, but which she also concedes can never be fully understood. There is an ineffable quality about the organic process of her work. Her finished prints have a "richness, translucency and liquidity that is an echo of the original glass form". The burnt impressions she effects are highly detailed and range in colour; "full of light with a mysterious photographic quality; in some areas they look as if they are backlit".

Gant's most recent body of work is influenced by her many travels across Europe, working as artist in residence Coordinator at Vrij Glas, in Zaandam, near Amsterdam, as well as visiting Italian ruins and traditional glass factories on the island of Murano in Venice, where she came into contact with traditional hand-made glass-blowing tools. As such, Gant is particularly inspired by the "piles and stacks of traditional Roman glass forms" that she found on these trips, and how to "connect these prints to their glass craft origins". It is the sense of antiquity that these forms dictate that the artist references in her work.

That feeling of ancient, dirt-covered pieces speaks not only to the ideas of preciousness of the original object, but also extends the meaning of the print when it is completed: the final prints are brown, crusty, and damaged, like an excavated shard.

Thus, Gant's prints gain significance as works in their own right while still intimating the lost objects that inspired them.

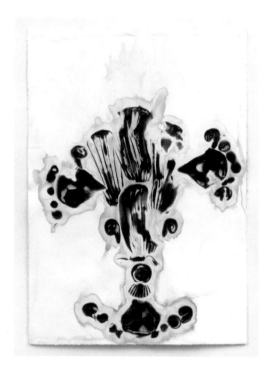

1

2

1 *Epergne 3*, circa 2000
Paper burned by hot glass.

2&3 *Midden and Moraine*,
circa 2000
Paper burned by hot glass,
228 x 304 cm.

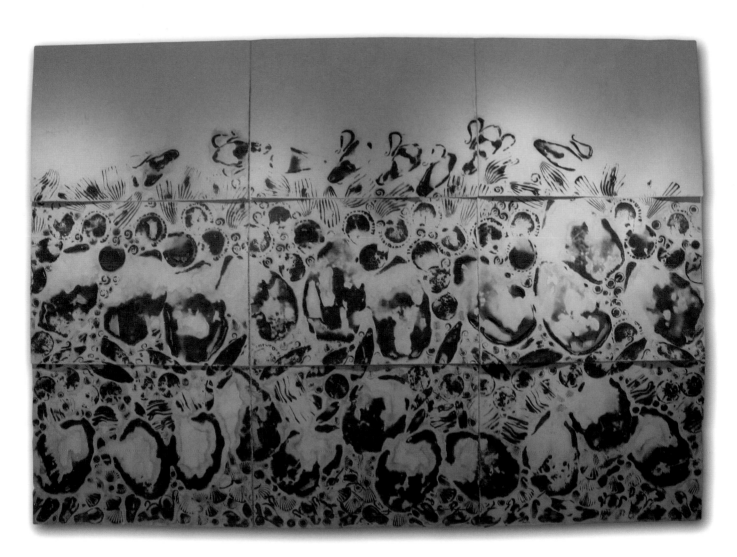

3

Michaela Nettell

Michaela Nettell attempts to capture in film the essential fleetingness and mutability of memory and dream, creating installations that explore the potential of projection techniques to affect relations of space, optics and memory. The filmic medium has often been discussed in relation to its oneiric qualities, and Nettell's work underscores this parallel both through its complex, layered visual material, and through enigmatic subject matter.

Nettell's 2007 piece, *Bathysphere*, exemplifies her interest in the illusionary possibilities of surface: five suspended glass spheres act as transparent and three-dimensional screens—or rather, receptacles—for sequences of film. Just as photographs might be seen to be the pictorial traces of the past, these fish-bowl apparatus become containers that literally possess or retain the fugitive image or dream. The female

subjects of the films swim underwater, blow bubbles and figure skate, expressions of fluidity and ephemerality that dissolve into the transparent materiality of the glass itself. The nebulous quality of glass is confirmed here, with the projected image causing its appearance to fluctuate between opacity and limpidity.

It is this relationship—between projected light and the materiality of glass—that forms the core of Nettell's work. Solitary, watery landscapes such as boats at sea, marshland and lakes illuminate the 'screens' to become part of them, the contours of the glass globes and the intangible moving images passing into each other to form a single, indefinite material.

While Nettell's glass spheres act as screens to be projected onto, they are also themselves able to project, as they

reflect their surroundings. This doubling permits the construction of an immersive environment for the piece, wherein layers of film, illusions and realities are blended to form an always different and indeterminate installation. To enter the space of *Bathysphere* is to become involved in its mercurial elements and imagined forms. In so doing, the viewer is able to bring their associations to the work, forming new, brief and impermanent narratives.

In this way, glass becomes the facilitator of an affective relationship with the viewer, enabling a space for contemplation that lies between the real and reverie. By situating glass between the facts of its transparency and its uncanny ability to become opaque Nettell is able to probe the line between what the eyes see and what the mind imagines.

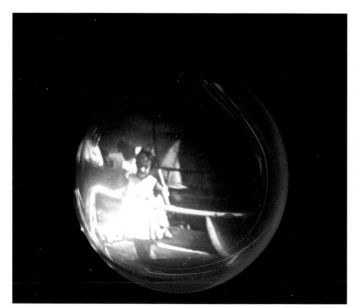

1

2

1&2 *Bathysphere* (details), 2007
Blown glass spheres, video,
15-22 cm in diameter.
Photographs by
Michaela Nettell.

3 *Bathysphere*, 2007
Blown glass spheres, video,
15-22 cm in diameter.
Photograph by Tom Simmons.

3

Tanja Pak

Born into a family of glass-blowers but influenced as much by industrial techniques and factory production processes, each element of Tanja Pak's artistic practice, from her large-scale installations to her functional designs for domestic use, reveals her mastery over the material. Pak's work in glass focuses on its most ethereal qualities, seemingly defying its own materiality.

There has long been a tradition of glass production in Slovenia, ever since the Venetians introduced glass-blowing to the country in the seventeenth century (commercial glass production has since become a major source of trade for the country). Yet Pak was the first Slovenian artist to use cast glass as a material for large-scale sculpture. In 1998 she responded to the architecture of Ljubljana Castle by producing a series of site-specific sculptures. Working with other glass specialists as well as light and audio technicians, she created *Voyage*, a series of glass rings suspended in a row from a barrel vaulted ceiling, a blue laser beam shot through the installation, representing what the artist describes as 'an infinite journey'.

In 2004 Pak installed *Traces* in the church of St Vit, Dravograd, KGLU Slovenj Gradec, Slovenia. The installation comprises a sequence of three sculptural interventions lining the nave of the church towards the altar in the apse. Using a combination of glass, metal and sand together with sophisticated lighting arrangements, each element of the installation creates a different atmospheric focus enhancing the contemplative effect of the venue.

For *Ponte dei Sospiri Lux Europae*, 2002, installed under a bridge in Copenhagen, Denmark, Pak referenced the famous Bridge of Sighs in Venice. Incorporating light and sound, the installation is made up of 220 glowing 'drops' of blown glass casting a serene reflection in the middle of a lake.

As well as exhibiting her work in glass in International Biennials and exhibitions, Pak works as a professor at The Academy of Fine Arts and Design in Ljubljana and runs Glesia Gallery in the same city in her native Slovenia. After studying industrial design at the Academy of Fine Arts also in Ljubljana, she went on to obtain a masters degree ceramics and glass from The Royal College of Art, London in 1996. She received Pilchuck scholarship in 1999 and in 2001 became a fellow at The Creative Glass Center of America in Pensilvania, America.

1

1 *Dreaming Away*, 2006
Cast crystal
glass, metal,
55 to 75 cm (three
different spheres.
Photograph by
Peter Koštrun.

2 *Traces*, 2004
Site-specific installation
using glass, metal, sand
and light.
Photograph by
Boris Gaberščik.

3 *Traces*, 2004
Site-specific installation
using glass, metal, sand
and light.
Photograph by
Boris Gaberščik.

2

3

4

4 *Ponte dei Sospiri,
Lux Europae*, 2002
Site-specific installation
using blown glass (220
drops), metal, light
and sound.
Photograph by Bent Ryberg.

5 *Traces*, 2004
  Site-specific installation
  using glass, metal,
  sand and light.
  Photograph by
  Boris Gaberščik.

George Papadopoulos

London-based artist George Papadopoulos is a designer that works with shattered glass panels, a technique he initially developed during his ceramics and glass studies at the Royal College of Art. These panels are comprised by laminated glass, a material which does not fall apart when shattered and whose fissures sparkle in unpredictable patterns. To these Papadopoulos adds colour and texture before covering the surface with more glass. He describes this process as a form of drawing: the 'marks' he makes combine spontaneity with control to an effect that is at once raw and refined.

Papadopoulos' company, Yorgos Studio, produces these one-off slices of colour and form for a range of public and private clients. They can be commissioned to fit into specific architectural spaces or to stand as individual pieces of art. The range is extremely diverse. Some consist of bold, minimal patterns, some are undeniably geological in appearance while others contain refracted figurative imagery, suggestive of the religious scenes of stained glass windows in churches. He explains:

In my work, I explore issues around the transparent and light-refracting qualities of glass when defining space. By combining the processes and techniques used in studio glass, I achieve inventive and exciting surface qualities. These effects become substantial building components which not only translate into a variety of contexts but can also serve a variety of functions.

Papadopoulos' work can be seen in the British Airways Terraces lounge at Heathrow airport, as well as various restaurants and offices. His murals have been exhibited at Cork Street Gallery, the Hellenic Centre in London, the Victoria and Albert Museum and the Henry Moore Gallery at the Royal College of Art. In 2004, A&C published Papadopoulos' manual, *Glass Lamination*, a guide to decorating glass involving such things as sandblasting and etching.

1

1 *Pool 1*, 2001
Glass, pigment, resin,
Five panels 240 cm x 70
cm (each).

2 *Red Hot Pokers*, 2003
Glass, pigment, resin,
40 x 61 cm.

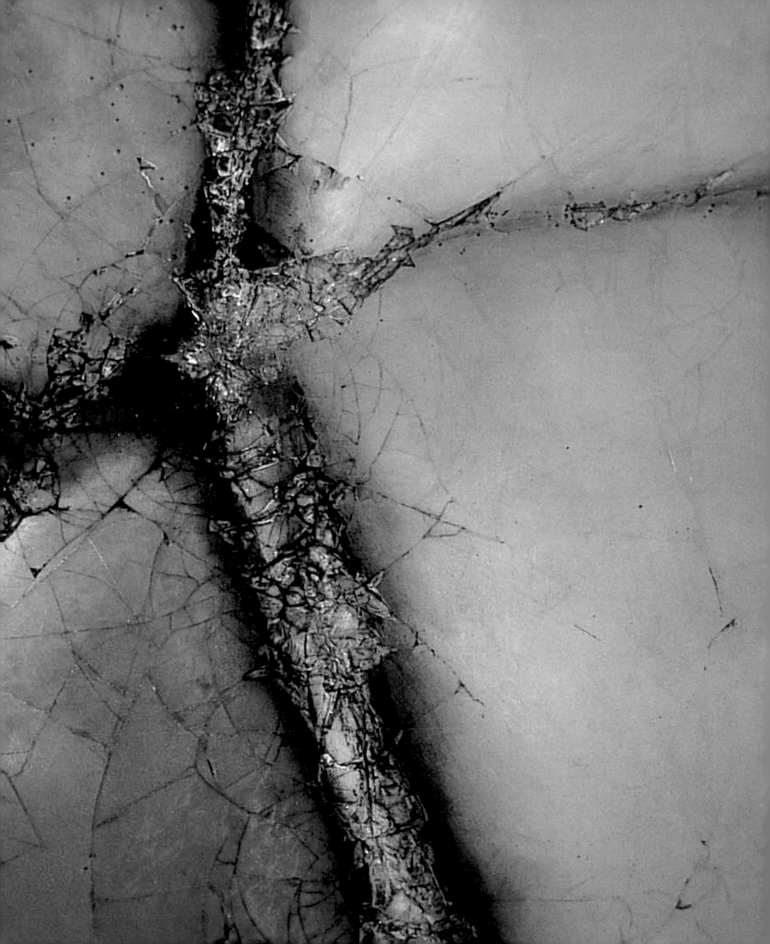

3 *Bath*, 2001
   Glass, pigment, resin,
   52 x 83 cm.

4 *Dissection*, 2006
   Glass, pigment, resin,
   six hanging panels,
   50 x 50 cm each.

George Papadopoulos

Tom Pearman

Tom Pearman is an artist whose work is as dynamic as it is eclectic. Treading the boundaries between furniture design, public art, printmaking, concrete sculpture, video and glass art his practice is concerned with the complexity and nuance of form, pattern and perspective, something that becomes manifest in his geometric and scientifically inspired screen prints overlaid onto a variety of media.

Pearman's glass pieces comprise both large-scale commissioned projects by such organisations as the Oxo Tower, the London Print Studio, the Crowbar Gallery, London and Broomfield Hospital, London, whose aesthetic tones echo those of the architectural spaces in which they are installed. The London Print Studio commission was, for example, printed onto 16 glass panels (140 x 16 centimetres each), and comprised vibrant blocks of colour which took the form of geometric boxes and lines, referring not only to the Studio space but also, via the use of printmaking, the technique that the work was constituted by. His glass 'artworks' are less grandiose in scale, depicting the minutiae of life in abstract shape and form. *Green Grass Flower*, 2003, takes what is a seemingly simple form, reconfiguring it into a geometric, letraset-style composition.

Pearman is interested by the opportunities proffered by printing onto glass to create depth of field and multiple layers. In the Crowbar Gallery installation, he installed four sheets of glass, one behind the other, each depicting architectural shapes and scenarios. Such an arrangement would allow the viewer to see all panels simultaneously, while offering a very different visual experience from each perspective—one that is seemingly in motion as colour and form collide. Works such as this not only speak of the materiality of the medium onto which he has printed but also of the processes involved in making them.

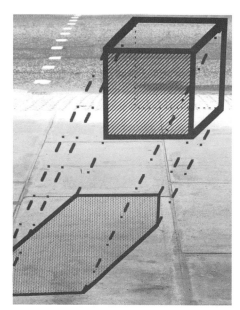

1

2

1&2 *London Print Studio Architectural Glass Commission*, 2000 Screenprint on 16 architectural glass panels, 1,400 x 650 cm each.

3 *Trickstar*, 2006 Fired enamel on glass, spray finished ply backing.

4 *Tricky*, 2006 Fired enamel on glass, spray finished ply backing.

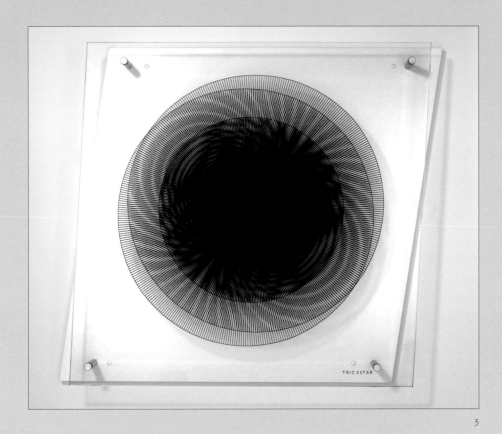

3

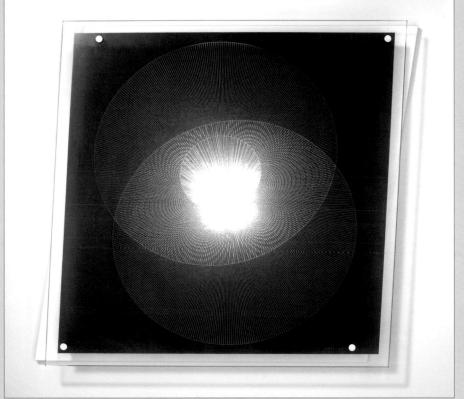

4

Deborah Sandersley

Deborah Sandersley's 'glass photographs' capture the changing landscapes of contemporary cities—particularly the streets of East London and the landscape gardens in the South of France—and fuse glass and photography to create more tangible, three-dimensional records of such scenes.

Working initially as a freelance photographer, Sandersley discovered the possibilities proffered by glass when a friend taught her to make stained glass windows. In so doing, she discovered that its properties could retain the three-dimensions which the photographic medium had failed to offer her and, by fusing, slumping and casting glass, was able to combine the two. Sandersley's images are largely concerned with the documentation of change in the urban landscape. Architecture, for all its fixedness, can communicate such changes; a factor that the artist exploits in her practice. She frequently photographs buildings and everyday scenes, and much of her recent work focuses on the urban scenes of the East East. "We are living through an age of accelerated evolution and architecture gives us a very vivid record of that process and one I try to capture in much of my work", she says. Working first with a camera, Sandersley screen prints photographs onto glass and then employs traditional and bespoke techniques—layering, shading and montage—to combine both disciplines. Once printed or fired with the photographic image, the glass is etched and often hand-painted. The transparency of glass captures light, which both creates depth and luminosity and refers back to the photographic medium from which the piece evolved.

1

1 *E2*, circa 2000
Screen-printed, etched
and hand painted glass
layers in wooden box with
integral coloured light,
83 x 60 x 12 cm.

2 *Hanbury Street*, circa 2000
Printed and etched glass
panelled box,
21 x 31 x 12 cm.

2

Elaine Sheldon

Elaine Sheldon's sculptures are the surprising consequence of imagined interactions between foreign and familiar items. She is concerned with exploring the material properties of glass, culminating in works (which are often fused with everyday objects) that are allowed to inflate freely and be affected by heat and gravity without resistance.

"Readymade, mass-produced objects intrigue me because they are forced into moulds—pressed, cast, stamped, drilled", says Sheldon.

The aesthetic of these objects is determined by a designer working within the limits of a manufacturing process and a particular material. I like the contrast between the aesthetic of these readymade objects and the

glass forms in my work that evolve during the making process. I am able to be led by the material but also to intervene.

Her best-known piece, *Bulldog Light*, 2003, is one of a series that plays with the purpose of everyday objects by fusing them with glass. A reinterpretation of the traditional pendant lamp, *Bulldog Light* is a glass lamp that appears to be suspended from a bulldog clip—rather than a usual rod or cord—which adopts a flesh-like quality where it is pinched beneath the clamp of the clip. This foray into combining glass with functional objects inspired another remarkable project, *Unsettled*, 2003—a set of chairs which grip and clamp freely inflated glass bubbles. Unlike *Bulldog Light* which, in blending glass and other objects, becomes a functional item, the marriage of

chair and glass makes the chairs impossible to sit on, and therefore useless.

Objects made of glass are usually perfect surfaces celebrating the smooth and polished surfaces which glass can form. Instead of trying to recreate such perfection, Sheldon's work explores the imperfect qualities of glassmaking. "Many of my glass pieces are inspired in part by the process of glass making", she claims:

I enjoy glass when it is allowed to move without encumbrance, and I attempt to accentuate this in some of my pieces, controlling a small area of the form while it is otherwise inflated freely.... The junction of the two is really refreshing.

1

1 *Unsettled*, 2003
Blown glass and wooden chairs, two elements, each element approximately 80 x 40 cm.

2 *Bulldog Light*, 2003
Blown glass and bulldog clip, 25 x 25 cm.
All photographs by Frank Thurston.

Helen Tiffany

Helen Tiffany is an artist inspired by the possibilities proposed by working with glass. She responds to the medium in its raw form and combines it with other materials such as metalwork. Tiffany describes her working process as "scientific", producing results that have been thoroughly researched, tried and tested and manipulated in their making. Of this approach she explains:

The beauty of glass is its versatility. It can take on solid form or be as thin as paper, it can be shaped and cut and polished but its most valuable asset is its translucency. I see glass as a visual medium, my pieces work with this ability to pass and diffuse light.

Glass Slides, 2007, typifies both 'science' and translucency. Comprising 12 'slides' in total, the artist has set work to make the piece Petri-dish-like in style. Made from transparent glass, each slide appears to contain organic matter at its centre. On closer inspection, revealed are colours, patterns and shapes that are both alien and abstract. These works are selected by 'image type' and then displayed in a number of ways, whether they large-scale projections, illuminations, or close-up viewing boxes.

By manipulating the way that such works can be viewed and by projecting light through and from them, Tiffany seeks to distort and challenge the way that glass is usually perceived. She states:

The slide format is ideal, allowing them to be used in a variety of ways including traditional projection. By passing light through the slide it changes how is perceived. It could be a large-scale painting or a stained glass window.

Many of Tiffany's pieces are interactive and encourage the viewer to touch the work on display. By providing such a myriad of experiences for the viewer the artist encourages the same proposition of experimentation and manipulation that she herself is so roused by.

1

1 *Glass Slides*, 2007
  Float glass fused with metal sheet
  (copper, brass, gilding metal, silver,
  steel and nickel),
  5 x 5 x 0.2 cm each.

2 *Steel*, 2007
  Float glass and steel.

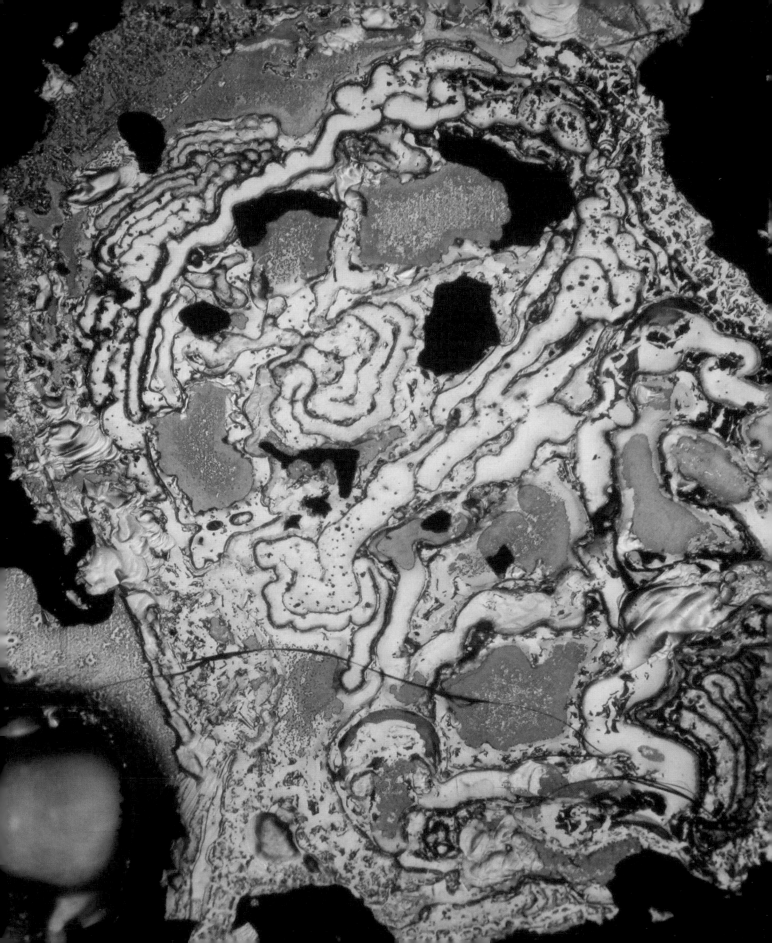

Mark Zirpel

Mark Zirpel is a Seattle-based artist working in glass and mixed media. His practice comprises an ongoing process of inquiry and discovery concerning the relationship between humanity's place and the universe. His approach is multi-disciplinary and concept driven, pushing the parameters of the medium beyond the decorative and the embellished. Magic, the alchemical transformation of the world through the transmutation of matter, and a belief in the interconnectedness of all things, are the guiding forces shaping Zirpel's art.

"There is a quality of the unknown in my work and a sense of investigation" Zirpel explains.

This occurs technically and conceptually. I am open to new information, new materials, and techniques. My work bridges disciplines.... I have focused on sculpture for the last 15 years as it offers an openness to approach, to materials, to its utilisation of space and light, to its non-pictorial qualities, to its power to communicate. It is experiential and sensual.

Zirpel's most recent work features kinetic sculpture. The series *Body Work* is a natural development from an earlier study of solar, lunar and tidal cycles, exploring the mechanics of the human form. The fragility of these delicate machines reminds us of bodies "labouring to continue functioning until their eventual demise". Creating the piece was a complex, open-ended process involving pneumatics, programmable microcontrollers, motion control, infrared sensors, rubber and glass casting, metal fabrications, complexly-timed mechanical apparatuses, thermo sensors, blown and kiln-formed glass and digital voice chips. *Water Organ* is a similar exploration of kinetic sculptural forms. Consisting of glass, water and steel, the piece is reminiscent of an eccentric scientific laboratory; the siphoning action of water continually pumps air, which in turn generates sound through the activation of reeds. Materials and techniques are once more freely explored in a multidisciplinary environment where the worlds of science and magic meet.

Zirpel has taken part in numerous international residencies, worked extensively with Pilchuck Glass School and exhibited widely. He was recently awarded the Stephen Proctor fellowship from the Australian National University in Canberra.

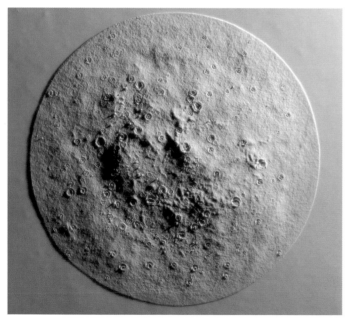

1

2

1 *Luna*, 2004
Kiln-formed glass,
48 x 48 x 2.5 cm.

2 *Projector*, 2003
Kiln-formed glass,
lead, oil, fire,
copper, steel,
40 x 80 x 120 cm.

3 *Eclipse*, 2004
Kiln-formed
glass, enamel,
48 x 48 x 3.7 cm.

4 *Black Luna*, 2003
Kiln-formed glass, salt,
75 x 120 x 5 cm.

3

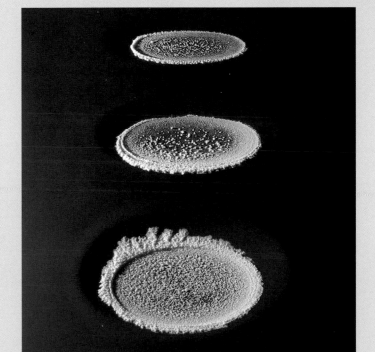

4

Installation

Through a Glass Darkly: Artists, Glass and Authorship

Michael Petry

Contemporary artists have long worked with craftsmen—from studio assistants to factory and foundry workers—to realise work that they would otherwise be unable to make. How can one then describe the work that results from this commonplace collaboration? Is it an artwork, or a piece of craft? It can be described as an artwork by virtue of being devised by an artist, but also can be thought of as properly belonging to craft, as it was made by a craftsperson. Who draws this distinction and why? How does this determination affect how the object is ultimately viewed, consumed and exhibited?

Marcel Duchamp 'made' his *Air du Paris*, 1919, before leaving Paris for America. Asking a pharmacist to empty a glass bottle containing a "physiological serum", the artist instructed him to fill it with air and seal it up again.[1] This, one of Duchamp's earliest readymades, is one of the most well-known examples of a glass work conceived by an artist but manufactured by someone else with greater technical skill. Could Duchamp have physically made the work? Perhaps, with time and effort, but that was not the point. Having introduced the notion of the readymade, Duchamp would enable other artists to follow suit, employing the skills of a collective, while still retaining 'authorship' of the artistic product. As a result, Duchamp introduced the twentieth century to a whole new way of thinking about 'making' art, one that purported that concept takes precedence over making.

Duchamp's readymades would raise the question of the (im)possibility of originality and of a single 'author' in the production of the art object. However, it was his contemporary, the French philosopher Roland Barthes, who really brought the concept into the creative consciousness in his highly influential text "Death of the Author".[2] Barthes suggested that, through the act of reading a text (or, for the purpose of our argument, viewing an artwork), it is the reader who writes the text, completing it through the very action of reading. He warns against considering the "author's" intention or personal history when reading a work, and rather maintains that the work exists outside of the personal context of the author, or indeed outside of any context at all.

This concept of the 'death of the author' proposed by Barthes, would soon give rise to debate concerning the 'rebirth of the author' and the dialectic that 'context' (whether it be the personal history of the artist, or the broader socio-economic circumstances at the time of making) could not be disregarded when considering works of art. This view of artistic production would hold sway particularly in the 1980s and 90s, leading to a counter-reformation of autonomy in art where artists would claim that they were indeed the 'authors' of their work, (regardless of who actually 'made' it).

As a result of the collaboration between craftsman and artist, the artist must at least acknowledge the level of skill that goes into making a piece of art. As Liam Reeves, chief glass technician at the Royal College of Art, recalls of his experience as a craftsman, "as a maker, you can be limited by your own ideas of the limits of the process and quite often (artists) will push you to do something you didn't think was possible.... It is a fine line between yes and no."[3] Such collaborations often mean that the role of the craftsman is in flux, especially as more makers begin to consider themselves artists in their own right. Asked how he conceives of his own work, Reeves claims that it is "strongly rooted in the tradition of making glass but [with] a conceptual edge" and when asked about the work he does for artists he replied with the one word answer; "art".

Mark Quinn terms the collaborative efforts between craftsman and artist as "improvisation". As he has said of his *The Etymology of Morphology*, 1996:

> [It was] made by glass-blowers in Murano who have a flawless grasp of their technique [and who use] their strengths to do something different. The pieces are blown in clear glass and then holes are drilled in the base and a craftsman, who silvers mirrors, silvers the inside.... It was created on the hoof, that is, I drew the shapes on a piece of paper and the glass-blower created them. It's a record of improvisation.[4]

This comment gives insight to Quinn's working process and how he perceives the relationship between himself, the 'artist', and those who actually make his work. Such works are, however, most often viewed by the art world as belonging to the artist rather than being the result of a collaborative process. Represented by the prestigious White Cube Gallery in London, Quinn's works are firmly located in the realm of 'art' rather than 'craft', though he has described his role as similar to "a director working with actors".[5] The concept of a theatrical means of production, involving the help of many skilled makers, he views as a vital part of his directorial vision.

Artist Kiki Smith has said "I love working with people who know more than I do" when asked about her relationship with the craftsmen she collaborates with.[6] Smith's work in glass encompasses blown glass, lampwork and glass engraving. She perceives the work produced by the craftsmen she collaborates with as an 'interpretation' of her initial concept. This is a view that many artists who work with craftspeople appear to share. In this type of relationship, two levels of translation occur. The artwork is initiated by the artist. The maker then re-translates this idea back into two- or three-dimensions, approximating the artist's vision. This double distance is what I, as an artist and writer, find most intriguing. For, in this relationship between artist and maker, the work of art is located primarily in the ether of thought, in the discourse between the artist and maker.

Smith takes a different approach when working with glass-blowers: "I like to make things that are neutral so that the hand of the glass-blower is not in the work. I usually use geometric shapes, so the pieces are not specific to the blowers."[7] This is evidenced in works such as *Tears*, 1994, *Red Spill*, 1996, or *Shed*, 1996, and those like *The Path to Hope*, 2006. In a manner not dissimilar to Quinn, her position is that of director striving to organise a myriad of elements into a coherent whole. Works by artists such as Smith aim to minimise the intentionality of the maker in their translation, to avoid any additional flourishes, interpretations or concepts to become apparent. Yet, according to Reeves, "there is always

Left:
Kiki Smith
Shed, 1996
Image courtesy of
PaceWildenstein.
Photograph by
Shoshana Wayne.

Right:
Cerith Wyn Evans
*IMAGE (Rabbit's Moon) by
Raymond Williams*, 2004
Black chandelier
(Barovier & Toso), flat
screen monitor, Morse
code unit and computer
Dimensions variable
© The artist.
Image courtesy Jay
Jopling/White Cube
(London).Photograph
by Andy Keate.

a fingerprint of the maker, even in a factory [when] two guys are blowing the exact same thing. (To a trained eye) you can pick out the difference and tell who made what".[8] So perhaps the translation that evolves between artist and maker is one more conversational than either might consciously realise.

Cerith Wyn Evans has long since used glass in his neon sculpture work, as well as in his series of chandeliers. Wyn Evans appropriates the text of writers, philosophers and poets at the initial stages of each of his works, translating these into his sculptural objects that bear his own stamp. Works like *Meanwhile Across Town*, 2001, or *Later That Day*, 2001, comprise neon glass tubes in various sized editions. Like the first editions of the books they are inspired by, Wyn Evans' works are multiples, whose production is finite. They read as both text and image, translating the concepts communicated by the book itself and Wyn Evans' own views concerning authorship.

Wyn Evans has also made a series of works where text is literally 'broadcast' into the gallery space by Morse Code. His *Rabbit Moon*, 2004, features an elaborate Murano glass chandelier, which pulses on and off as the text is transmitted. Unless the viewer understands Morse Code, they cannot decipher the words communicated by the flashing chandelier; they are left in the dark, so to speak, with only the rhythm of the blinking lights interrupting an otherwise opaque environment.

Liliane Lijn has stated: "You should never make anything somebody else can make. I only make the things that nobody but me can make."[9] This attitude to production has been a stance she has held since the early 1960s, which caused her "no end of trouble" at the time. Many artists and curators have felt she was somehow cheating, yet the same critics did not chastise Donald Judd or Richard Serra for working with foundries and factories. Lijn was expected, like Eva Hesse, to 'make' her own work. Lijn has actively worked to counteract gender casting and her kinetic sculptures and mechanised installations require a wide variety of collaborators, many of whom are based in the traditionally 'male' realm of scientific enquiry. She is well-known for her huge cone-shaped structures that incorporate a number of materials, and has used a wide variety of 'masculine' materials such as bronze and steel in her work. In *Divided Self*, 2001, from the series *Bodyscapes: Dreaming Oneself*, she combines cast glass with argon onto patinated bronze and stainless steel.

Mona Hatoum, on the other hand, has embraced the production aesthetic in her work *Drowning Sorrows*, 2001–2002. Here mass production plays a double role in the manufacture of the art-object. In this piece Hatoum scatters wine bottles to form a circle on the floor. They appear broken but have, in fact, been meticulously cold worked to stand at odd angles. While

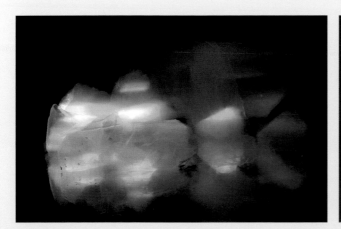

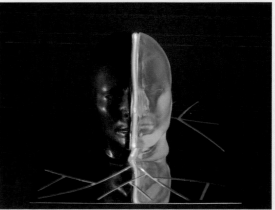

their arrangement seems random, they have been deliberately placed in accordance with Hatoum's artistic vision. Despite being mass-produced these bottles were all individually worked and, making the piece into an edition of three, simply reinforces the notion of mass production evident elsewhere in the piece. All the same, the invisible fingerprints of the glass workers are there, as is the machine's imprint in the bottom of each bottle. In a most elegant 'green' moment of recycling, Hatoum makes an artwork that speaks of its own production as an artwork and as a mass produced piece.

Her largest work in glass *Web*, 2006–2007, features hundreds of clear blown glass orbs suspended like giant dew drops on a spider web. First installed in Italy, it was then transferred to London's White Cube in 2007. Visitors were allowed to walk within the huge web but not to touch the glass (from fear of breakage). The 'author' of this work is incontestable; while the glass orbs and steel wire may have been constructed by others, there is no apparent 'interpretation', this piece most certainly carries Hatoum's stamp.

Jorge Pardo is an artist who deliberately blurs the ground between architecture, design, craft and fine art in his large-scale pieces, making untitled installations that often look like furniture or lighting installations. While much of this work is installation art, most pieces can be re-sited into different dimensions and locations. His *Untitled Installation I*, 1999, is a perfect example of how a work at first appears to be mass-produced, but is, in fact, unique. The objects comprising the installation are familiar and yet odd, they come in multiples which, when combined, make a unique whole that is in itself variable and changeable adapting to different sites in its physical layout. He adds to the confusion by using functional mass produced objects, altering and fusing them with his own designs. The 'hand' of the factory is silent. The works present themselves as designed products, yet are perceived by the art world largely as installation.

Like Wyn Evans, Pardo investigates what it means to be an 'author' of a piece of work, appropriating 'readymade' glass products to constitute a broader whole. Smaller installations like *Untitled Installation*, 2005, might be more likely to find their way into the home of a collector as opposed to a museum (where many of the larger pieces eventually reside) but have the same principle of creation.

Jennifer Bartlett is best known for her seemingly simple paintings of houses and structures, often choosing to work with a grid system. She uses minimal means to create dense visual patterns that are simultaneously abstract and evocative of figuration. The marks themselves are often a veil through which light passes. In her installation for the St Steven Episcopal Church in Houston, Texas, eight windows form the emotive backdrop to the church's

Left:
Mona Hatoum
Drowning Sorrows
2001-2002
Glass bottles
10 x 250 cm
© The artist.
Image courtesy Galerie
Rene Blouin, Montreal and
Jay Jopling/White Cube
(London). Photograph by
Richard-Max Tremblay.

Right:
Jorge Pardo
Untitled installation,
1999
70 Glass Lamps
(cobalt blue),
dimensions variable.
Image courtesy of
Haunch of Venison.

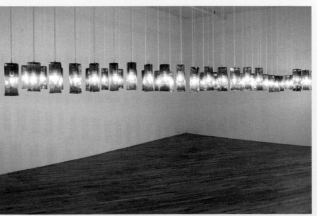

Collundarium, a place where the ashes of the departed members of the congregation are stored. Her scheme was developed from her Homanji windows for the American National Airport, which were based on a series of drawings she made for a temple in Japan. Bartlett's abstracted images have a power of their own, yet allow the needs of the congregation to be satisfied without overwhelming the integrity of the project. It is as if the viewers—whether spiritual or not, whether secular or not—can see through her glass darkly taking with them the unique uplift that art can provide.

It is the work that survives, the discourse and disgruntled voices about whether craft and art are in the same game, or even whether it is still possible for there to be an 'author' to the object at all. As more and more artists blur the artificial (mainly Western) boundaries between what is made, and by which class of artisan (artist versus craftsperson) does that making, those distinctions become less important and might eventually fall away. Who a glass craftsperson makes art for is no longer the question. Perhaps the real work of art is embedded in the concept that underpins it (rather than its physical manifestation) and in how it is perceived by the viewer. Whether glass objects are art or craft seems only to be an economic distinction; people still pay much more for art. In the end, it is the experience of all those fingerprints, singular or collective, that ultimately impact upon the viewer.

1   Schwarz, Arturo, *The Complete works of Marcel Duchamp*, London: Thames and Hudson, 1997, p. 676.
2   Barthes, Roland, "The Death of the Author", *Image-Music-Text*, New York: Hill and Wang, 1978.
3   Interview with Liam Reeves by the author January 11, 2008.
4   Mark Quinn cited in *Sara Whitfield in conversation with Mark Quinn*, Tate Liverpool.
5   Mark Quinn cited in *Sara Whitfield in conversation with Mark Quinn*, Tate Liverpool.
6   Interview with Kiki Smith by the author, October 22, 2007.
7   Interview with Kiki Smith by the author, October 22, 2007.
8   Interview with Liam Reeves by the author January 11, 2008.
9   Interview with Liliane Lijn by the author January 9, 2008.

Jeff Bell

Jeff Bell is a Yorkshire-born artist who creates unique sculptural and architectural pieces in cast glass. His pieces range from baths and crystal towers to the development of textured glass panels that envelope entire buildings. Bell continuously pushes the boundaries of the medium through his unique, aesthetically engaging installations and introduces new meanings and dimensions to the architectural space in which exhibits them. Modern yet rooted in the tradition of craftsmanship, his designs have gained widespread acceptance and can be seen in various public, private and corporate buildings across London, Berkshire and elsewhere.

My pieces consist of raw glass sheets or ingots, often coloured with enamels, which are placed onto sculpted plaster and fired in the kiln. At these extreme temperatures the molten glass takes on the shape and texture of his carved moulds. Due to the nature of kiln-formed process every piece of glass develops its own inner landscape of colours, forms and patterns. The work, after several days, finally emerges from the kiln with a life of its own.

Bell responds to each commission collaboratively with his clients, a process that is an essential element of his approach to artmaking. His work includes projects as diverse as an illuminated glass stair screen, a four metre high sculptured vortex of embossed crystal bowls, and three-storey high glass 'water-dragon' fountain.

Bell holds a BA Honours degree in three-dimensional design from Buckinghamshire College and has since worked in conjunction with leading architects internationally. In 1986 he set up his own studio. His work has been widely praised by the international design press and media. In 1993 Bell was awarded the RIBA Art in Architecture Award and in 1998 invited to exhibit in the prestigious Crafts Council Glass Light and Space exhibition.

1

1 *Canopy*, 2006
Suspended light
sculpture,
200 x 270 x 100 cm.

2 *Site Oxshot*, 2000
Old Street Cured Screen,
250 x 600 x 240 cm.
Image courtesy
of J Richards.

3 *Shoal*, 2001
Slumped toughened glass
(illuminated) at Arts
Space, Sheffield,
320 x 270 cm.

2

3

Richard Box

Initially trained as a sculptor at the Winchester School of Art in the early 1990s, it was not until 2001 that Richard Box began to work in neon glass. After a residency at the Bristol University Physics Department in 2003, he acquired the necessary skills of glass-blowing and vacuum technology to start work on his epic site-specific installations of light. His first foray into such installation work was the *Field* project, comprised by 1,301 152 centimetre fluorescent tubes. Box harnessed the electromagnetic field produced by the overhead power lines in order to power the neon lights. The piece was interactive, allowing people to ebb and flow through the space. Such interaction impacted on the properties of the piece itself—disrupted the electromagnetic field thus making the "visible, invisible".

Works such as *Field* not only transform when intercepted by the viewer but also affect the spaces in which they are installed. What were once seemingly barren and uninteresting landscapes acquire a third dimension when illuminated by the light emanating from the piece. Other projects in which Box has deployed neon lighting include *Electric Fluid*, 2007, and *Shake Pole*, 2006, encompassing 793 and 831 fluorescent tubes retrospectively, and which are just as ambitious in scale.

Box has continued to develop his skills in glass-blowing, culminating in smaller-scale projects, such as those at Spike Island, a fully functional glass retail outfir. He continues to push the technology and limits of cold cathode lighting, lathe work and glass-blowing.

1

2

1&3 *Electric Fluid*, 2007
Site-specific installation
comprising 793 fluorescent tubes.
2,150 x 270 x 150 cm.

2 *Shake Pole*, 2006
Site-specific installation
comprising 831 fluorescent tubes,
1,450 x 390 x 150 cm.
All photographs by Peter Dibdin:
www.peterdibdin.com

3

Kirsty Brooks

Describing herself as an "architectural glass artist" Kirsty Brooks has worked on a variety of commissions for public, private and corporate clients in a number of architectural environments. Using glass and screen prints to create walls, canopies, screens, windows and feature panels, she works in close collaboration with architects, interior designers and the clients to create site-specific work that responds to the context and history of the space in question.

The visual dialogue she effects between a building and its history is evidenced by such designs as the facade of the Look Ahead Housing and Care office, which features images of London housing taken in bygone eras, and a project involving the architecture of Chance de Silva, where she superimposed images of antiquated stairwells on the fabrication of a Victorian terrace.

The range of techniques Brooks employs in her practice allows her work to be both nuanced and varied while still maintaining a unique aesthetic. The contemporary techniques she employs throughout her practice paradoxically allow such composites to blend into the historical context of the space without visually dominating the surrounding architecture.

As well as Site-specific commissioned work, Brooks has also exhibited across Europe in shows such as Fragile Cargo, 2004–2005 which toured Hungary, England and Belgium, and Nou Vitrall, 2003, Barcelona.

1

1 *Treading the Boards, The Grand Opera House Belfast, 2006*
Screen printed glass enamel on float glass, 2690 x 80 x 2.1 cm.
Photograph by Philip Vile.

2 *Glass Artwork for Cargo Fleet, 2004*
Digitally printed etch and clear vinyl on float glass, 150 x 150 x 2.5 cm.
Photograph by Philip Vile.

3 *Financial Services Authority Restaurant Screens, 1999*
Screen printed etch vinyl on float glass, 229 x 158 x 1.2 cm.

2

3

Nick Crowe

At the core of Nick Crowe's diverse artistic practice is an interest in the latent ideologies embedded within technologies of various types, and the often-contingent frameworks upon which they are constructed. For Crowe, glass becomes a sculptural medium through which to convey the politics of these 'high-tech' media, and their social implications; both globally and locally.

The inherent dualities of glass—its fluid transparency and solidity, its fragility and hardness—permit Crowe to reveal the ambiguities that underlie the dissemination of information in the world. As both subject and object, Crowe uses glass to point toward the materiality of its form, and to demonstrate the socio-political applications of industrial glass. In other works, Crowe has utilised the Internet as a material in itself, manipulating this most contemporary of mediums to create temporally situated, ephemeral works that in their very essence touch upon the questionable nature of information transmission.

Operation Telic, 2005–2006 for example, consists of 12 glass panels, each showing an image of the ongoing Iraq War. Photographs taken from the Ministry of Defence website, they have been pared down to comic book-style outlines and hand-etched onto float glass. Lit from underneath, the glass panels can appear like small memorial tablets, but simultaneously evoke the image display of a night vision device. It is this duality that Crowe's work explores: *Operation Telic* does not sit simply as a condemnation of the glorification of war, but rather explores the subversive line between such images as objective documents of events, and as fully subjective propaganda.

In another recent piece, *The Campaign for Rural England*, 2006, Crowe demonstrates the integral engineering of contemporary glass materials: a full-sized bus shelter has undergone an attack of vandalism to reveal the properties of its toughened glass. Unexpectedly, however, the crystalline fragments formed through its shattering have not crumbled but instead have been left suspended, frozen in the instant of its destruction. Such works carry within them the ideological frameworks of their construction; an inherent weakness and innocuousness that belies its alternatively incisive, knife-like qualities. Crowe's work is thus unified by his ability to reveal the dual and varied effects of industrially fabricated glass, situated often between its destructive and creative possibilities.

1

2

1&2 *The Beheaded*, 2006
Ceiling mounted
mobile with armatures
of powder-coated mild
steel, suspending 68
elements cut from
0.3 cm dichroic
glass with Kevlar
thread, 320 cm aerial
circumference with
280 cm drop.

3 *The Campaign for Rural England*, 2006
English Oak with three
layer, 1.5 cm laminated
toughened safety glass
(cracked and bonded),
410 x 240 x 160 cm.

4 *Three Cynical Objects*, 2001
UV-bonded float glass set
in white American ash,
19 x 53 x 19 cm.
All photographs by
David Williams.

3

4

Stuart Haygarth

Stuart Haygarth is a London-based designer/ artist whose oeuvre is comprised by the re-use of everyday objects. Transcending the boundaries between photography, installation, sculpture and product design Haygarth's works utilise everyday objects, such as vessels, glasses and bottles which he reconfigures to form new and innovative designs—once defunct or useless, in such combinations they acquire a new significance.

Aladdin, 2006, for example, is a collection of glassware salvaged from flea markets, car boot sales and junk shops. Lovingly restored and arranged in glass vitrines according to their colour, the goblets, vases and platters regain their original lustre within amber, green, purple and clear groupings.

Other works tread a similar line. *Shadey Family*, 2004, for example, a linear chandelier constituted by recycled glass lampshades works to transform seemingly uninteresting objects by becoming an entirely different entity when viewed collectively. In a similar vein, *Spectacle*, 2006, is a second chandelier design constructed by prescription glasses that are linked together. As Haygarth explains: "By using prescriptive spectacles which were once an essential tool for seeing, an interesting analogy is drawn between their old and new purposes."

Pushing this concept further is *Optical*, 2007, another chandelier that encompasses over 4,500 prescription spectacle lenses hung on a monofilament line from a platform. The artists draws parallels between this piece and a mirror ball, whose appeal derives from the fact that it refracts rather than reflects light.

Haygarth worked as visiting lecturer at Plymouth University Photography Department, from 1995–2005. It was during this period that he commenced making works in glass. Such is his influence, that he has numerous clients including Porsche, Daimler Chrysler, Honda, Ernest & Julio Gallo Wines, Sony, Compaq, Patek Philippe, Natwest Bank, Norwich Union, British Midland Airways, Beggars Banquet Records, XL Records, The BBC, *The Times*, *GQ Magazine*, and Harper Collins Publishing to name but a few.

1

1&2 *Aladdin*, 2006
Installation at
Designersblock,
London. Photograph
by Jeff Leyshon.

Following pages:
Optical (large), 2007
MDF, monofilament line,
prescription
spectacle lenses, 150 cm
in diameter.

Mike Kelley

Mike Kelley began making his colourful glass sculptures and installation pieces in the late 1970s, when he moved to California to complete an MFA at the California Institute of the Arts. He then settled in Los Angeles, where he still lives and works today. Originally from Detroit, Kelley's work explores his childhood memories, which he refers to as "memory ware", using found fragments of family china, coloured glass shards, and ceramic waste.

Kelley has a pluralistic approach to art, appropriating the debris of Americana and pop culture from the past and present, as well as excavating more personal memory fields from his suburban upbringing. The horrors he dredges up and casts in glass include photos from high school yearbooks, snow globes, old rusting badges, cartoon characters, advertising brands; all gathered together in varying forms of encrusted, shiny, gummi-bear like forms.

Kelley's work is infused with references to myths and symbols from across the twentieth century, exploring subjects as diverse as the musical experiments of Russian composer Alexander Scriabin to Superman's hometown in his recent project *Kandors*, 2007. Kelley also cites Sylvia Plath as an inspiration behind his glass domes, which are direct interpretations of the ominous metaphorical 'Bell Jar' taken from her novel of 1963. These perfect domes are hand-blown in the Czech Republic and then tinted in America with a palette ranging from garish orange to leafy green to pale violet, creating an overall effect of a "night-club designer having been unleashed in a gallery" as German critic, Holger Liebs, describes.

Kelley's interpretations of other artists' works tread a thin line between homage and parody. However, his yoking together of Superman and bell jars is undertaken with complete focus and attention (even if they are coated with his ubiquitous shine and luminosity); revealing them as inseparable, necessary parts of the great imagination of contemporary popular culture.

Kelley is an iconic glass artist whose work has been collected and exhibited all over the world. He has received many awards, including the Wolfgang Hahn Prize, 2006, and the John Simon Guggenheim Memorial Foundation Fellowship, 2003.

1

1 *Kandor 4*, 2007
Mixed media with
video projection,
dimensions variable.

2 *Kandor 7*, 2007
Mixed media
with video,
dimensions variable.

Following pages:
Kandor 6, 2007
Mixed media with
video projection,
dimensions variable.

All images courtesy
of Jablonka Galerie,
Cologne/Berlin.
All photographs by
Fredrik Nilsen.

Danny Lane

Danny Lane has worked as a glass designer in London since the 1980s. His glass works are both diverse in form and varied in scale, ranging from small-scale furniture through to monumental installations for architectural spaces. He counts as his contemporaries Tom Dixon and Ron Arud who, along with Lane himself, were highly influential in the avant-garde furniture movement of the 1980s.

Lane's most well-known glass furniture designs include his *Etruscan* and *Stacking Chairs*, both of which of which incorporate broken glass in their design. His largest sculpture to date, *Borealis*, 2005, which is situated at the GM Renaissance Center, Detroit, is the biggest glass installation in the world.

Borealis epitomises the designer's preoccupation with creating works that are both monumental and brutal in design. In it, he combines broken, cracked glass with rusting and twisted steel, thus commenting on the transience of such elements, while also aiming to speak of the heightened experience of the viewer as they come into contact with such works.

Initially trained as a painter, drawing is an integral part of Lanes' practice, his concepts evolving from the drawing board through to its two- and three-dimensional realisation.

Not all of Lane's work is located in the realm of the grandiose, however. Works such as *Goldfish*, circa 2000, a kiln-formed colour glass bowl only measures at 27 x 77 x 74 centimetres. Even in these works, Lane's preoccupation with challenging the materiality of the medium is evident. Twisted, fractured and deconstructed, this piece only serves to strength the message implicit in the designer's oeuvre.

Lane's commissions include projects for Jesus College, Cambridge, Borgholm Castle, Sweden, and the National Assembly for Wales. His work can be found in collections and museums worldwide.

1

1 *Broken Bench*, 2004
 Glass, stainless steel,
 42.6 x 224 x 42 cm.
 Photograph by Peter Wood.

2 *Parting of the Waves*, 2003
 Glass and stainless steel sculpture,
 400 x 1,110 cm (each wall).
 Photograph by Peter Wood.

3

3 *Against the Wall*, 2001
Glass and steel sculpture,
250 x 800 x 80 cm.
Photograph by Peter Wood.

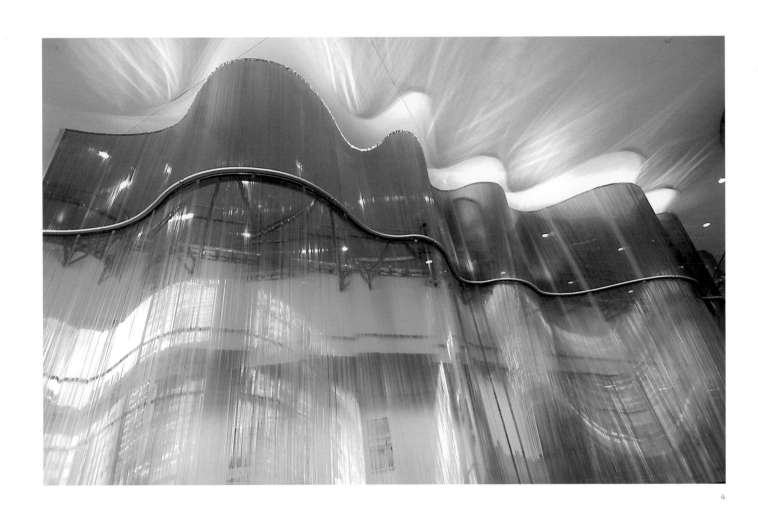

4 *Borealis*, 2005
  Glass and steel sculpture,
  640 x 1,820 cm (east wall)
  40 x 1,700 cm (west wall).

Danny Lane

Silvia Levenson

Glass is not a neutral material, but a very powerful medium of communication. I see it as a metaphor for transparency, for feeling and revealing emotions. It is a wonderful material that is both beautiful and treacherous.

Silvia Levenson's kiln-cast glass objects explore the uneasiness of domestic, everyday life, transforming the home into a site of struggle, tension, violence and love. "Sometimes households become like a pressure cooker" Levenson states.

Houses are cosy milieux that often turn into small emotional time bombs. My current work investigates family relationships where a subtle, but clearly visible, violence exists.

In the tradition of artists such as Annette Messager and Mike Kelley, Levenson infuses the everyday and the quotidian with a dark, subtle humour and a rather disquieting subject matter. Levenson explores the tensions and contradictions inherent in everyday life, and dwells beneath appearances to uncover the hidden and the unconscious: children shoes and female bags become dangerous objects equipped with pins and razor blades; pink high heels are spiked with wires; medicine cabinets are stocked with pink guns.

Glass perfectly encapsulates the contradictions Levenson explores. "I use glass as a narrative medium.... Glass is strong and fragile, hot and cold. I am fascinated by this ambiguity" she explains.

Realising objects, I investigate my life, my past and what is around me. I evoke political events, such as the Argentinean dictatorship and migrations, my own origins (my grandmother and father emigrated to Argentina from Russia) and finally, the stresses in daily life.

Levenson fled from her home in Buenos Aires during the political upheavals of the 'dirty war' and immigrated to Italy where she currently lives and works. Her work has gained international acclaim and several of her pieces are included in prominent glass collections such as the Altare Glass Museum in Italy, the Glas Museum Frauenau in Germany and the Corning Museum of Glass, New York.

1

2

1 *Life is Beautiful*, circa 2006   2 *Little Ulysses*, 2006
PVC, kiln-cast, glass oars.
Photograph by Endos.

2

3

4

3 *Sit Down Please*, 2002
Kiln-cast glass/steel,
130 x 30 x 30 cm.
Image courtesy of Caterina
Tognon, Italy.

4 *Riguardati (take care of
yourself)*, 2003
Glass fused/mixed media,
180 x 200 x 60 cm.
Image courtesy of
The Bullseye Connection
Gallery, America. Photograph
by Natalia Saurin.

5 *Life Strategies*, 2008
Kiln-cast glass,
chair, video,
170 x 170 x 80 cm.
Photograph by Natalia Saurin.

Silvia Levenson

John Luebtow

John Luebtow's glass sculptures have a commanding presence. Originally working as a ceramic artist, Luebtow began exploring the potential of glass in the 1970s, striving for a medium that would allow him to expand his ideas and the scale of his works into the architectural arena. This dream has been realised in the number of large-scale glasswork sculptures that he has been commissioned to produce. Though often monumental in scale, his installations segue with the formal composition of the architectural landscapes they inhabit, highlighting and often mimicking the dimensions and line of the given space through their own fluid linearity and striated pattern-work.

Employing the elemental simplicity of naturally occurring forms, particularly the wave-form—prominent in the epic sheet glass installation *Linear Fountain*, 1988—his works evince a strongly conceptual, almost Brancusian fascination with the repetition and engagement of line and form in their realisation that gestures beyond naturally occurring materiality to ideas of time and infinity. Evolving from his drawings of the female nude, Luebtow's sculptures possess a calming sensibility that the delicate tone and translucence of his medium allows.

Glass is one of the few materials that allows the viewer to see the interior and exterior of an object simultaneously, thus in Luebtow's practice, what could seem densely overbearing if rendered in concrete, retain a legibility and visual modesty that defy their gargantuan size. *I-Beam*, 2008, illustrates just how Luebtow's works accentuate rather than dominate their architectural surroundings; the sharp geometry of the steel girder tempered by the undulating, rhythmic line of the wave-form and the striated, aquamarine glass highlighted by the natural light against its grey background. In contrast, the frenetic *Post-Twentieth Century: Linear Form Series*, 1985—with its fiercely diagonal cross-hatching and sand-blasted lines and dramatic spot-lighting—sees Luebtow playfully underscore and echoing the darkness and chaotic marbling present in the tiled floor.

As well as the large body of his publicly and privately commissioned work on display around the world, Luebtow has devoted much of his career to teaching art in his native California where he lives and works. He has exhibited widely both in California and across the US as well as in Europe. His works were included in the *Made in California: 1900-2000* exhibition at LACMA (Los Angeles County Museum of Art), 2001.

1

1 *Post-twentieth Century: Linear Form Series*, 1985
Kiln-formed glass, marble, light, polished stainless steel,
360 x 720 x 1,080 cm.

2 *Linear form I-Beam Series*, circa 1980s
Kiln-formed glass, steel I-Beam,
320 x 36 x 36 cm.

2

Katrin Maurer

The written word and the subtle ways in which people communicate with each other, both verbally and non-verbally, form the underlying theme in Katrin Maurer's work. Glass provides an ideal medium for the expression of her ideas. As a transparent material it evokes the unseen and the unacknowledged. "Working with transparent glass is like working with something which is not really there—an almost invisible solid", she says. And yet this fragile, translucent material is inherently dangerous too, for it can cut and injure and, as such, it becomes a metaphor for the hidden threats to which we may unknowingly be exposed.

In much of her work, Maurer explores the relationship between the seen and the unseen, the spoken and unspoken, by imposing words and images on various glass objects. The texts invite the viewer to touch and play with these objects, reading and reinterpreting the seemingly random collection of texts and visual elements which they bear and thus drawing their own narrative inferences from them.

In *Spectacle*, for example, 17 hanging glass objects, engraved with words and images, become transparent carriers of information, reflecting women's medical experiences over time and changing the viewer's perceptions as the pieces move. Relating to the Chernobyl nuclear disaster, *1986* recalls the artist's own childhood memory of being "under the contaminated cloud". In this, 195 moveable glass plates, supported by a stainless steel frame, present contradictory information about the event, while the material itself—transparent glass— symbolises the invisibility of radioactivity.

Combining words with sculptural forms, Maurer's works are three-dimensional narratives. She has exhibited widely in The Netherlands, Germany, Austria and Britain, as well as in South Africa, has won or been shortlisted for various art prizes, and has featured in a number of publications. Examples of her work are displayed in public collections at De Interpolis Kunstcollectie, Tilburg, and the Glasmuseum, Leerdam, in The Netherlands, and in Germany at the Glasmuseum Alter Hof Herding in Coesfeld-Lette.

1

1 *1986*, 2007
195 glass elements, stainless
steel frame, aluminium, nylon,
200 x 150 x 150 cm.
Photograph by
Clemens Karlhuber.

2 *1986*, 2007
195 glass elements, stainless
steel frame, aluminium, nylon,
200 x 150 x 150 cm.

3

Contemporary Glass

3 *The Spectacle* (detail), 2006
Glass, steel wire.

162

4 *The Spectacle,* 2006
Glass, steel wire.
All photographs by Ron Zijlstra.

Michael Petry

Texan-born Michael Petry is a multi-media artist, writer and curator who has lived and worked in London since 1981. His work is characterised by the highly aestheticised presentation of his installation-based art, which focuses on issues relating to homosexuality. Using media as diverse as glass, leather, wood, velvet and freshwater pearls his installations—through slight and very deliberate changes in form, colour and media—reveal a subversive and often innuendo-laden critique of standardised values concerning beauty, taste, sexuality and love.

His 2007 exhibition at Sundaram Tagore, entitled America the Beautiful, was a response to both the American invasion of Iraq and the country's stance in relation to homosexuality in the Armed forces—tying in issues of patriotism, love, conformity and identity. Working predominantly in glass and using a restricted palette of red, white and blue, his glass works ranged in technique and style; from the blown glass pieces *The Axis 2007*, and *Crocodile Tears*, 2007, to the *Broken Promises' Series*, 2007, comprised by large, interlocking glass rings.

Though he is best known for his large-scale installations, recent works such as *Lovers: The Bareback Series*, 2006, have seen Petry take a more intimate approach to his practice. Appropriating Victorian silver-plated occasional dishes by fusing them with poured molten glass, these new 'coupled' objects act as a metaphor for sexual intercourse; the delicate ornaments harbouring both the ideal of sex as the physical act of love between two people, as well as the pejorative associations surrounding unprotected sex.

As well as being represented and exhibited by Sundaram Tagore, New York, and Devin Borden Hiram Butler Gallery, Houston, and the Westbrook Gallery, London, Petry's works are included in prominent public collections throughout the world including the British Museum, London, the Museum of Arts and Design, New York, the Kunst und Ausstellungshalle der Bundesrepublick Deutschland, Bonn and the Bellerive Museum, Zurich.

1

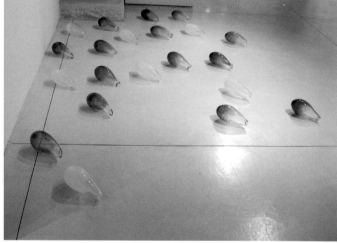

2

1 *5 Star*, 2007
Blown Glass.

2 *Crocodile Tears*, 2007
Dimensions variable.

3 *The Treasure of Memory*,
2000–2008
Collection of the Museum of
Arts and Design, New York.
Photograph by Per
Christian Brown.

4 *The Treasure of Memory*
(detail), 2000–2008
Collection of the Museum of
Arts and Design, New York.
Photograph by David Grandorge.

4

5

5 *BB62* from the *Bare Back
Lovers Series*, 2006
Molten glass poured into
silver-plated Victorian objects.
UK Government Art Collection.

6 *BB59* from the *Bare Back
Lovers Series*, 2006
Molten glass poured into
silver-plated Victorian objects.
Collection of Berverly and
Howard Robinson.

Michael Petry

Tobias Rehberger

Tobias Rehberger's installation work transposes our experiences of domestic environments and highstreet commerce into the gallery in order to propose questions concerning scale and taste. What makes something timeless? How do the objects we own, be it a sofa, car or TV, confer status on our lives?

Rehburger's practice straddles design and fine art disciplines giving precedence to contextual concerns of the exhibition venue. As well as his designs for interior environments his characteristically 'outside the box' approach has been applied to mural paintings, video work, sculpture and landscaping.

Some of Rehberger's most well-known glass works include the exterior passage way in Colle di Val d'Elsa, Tuscany, in which the artist installed a network of 150 locally produced glass ceiling lamps activated by an Internet link that monitored the sunrise and sunset in Montevideo.

Another renowned piece is the glass work he constructed for the exhibition, One, in 1995. In this piece he made a series of vases that embodied his relationship with his immediate circle of friends. The materials he used varied from a hollowed out tree-trunk to clay and glass. Friends were later invited to interact with the works.

Rehberger's practice can be seen to explore our, often intimate, relationship with objects. It is this surplus value—beyond material value—that informs his investigations and makes his work so relevant to discussions about the role of art in contemporary society.

Rehberger was born in Esslingen, Germany in 1966 and now lives in Frankfurt. He has exhibited widely including major shows at Reina Sofia, Madrid, Whitechapel Art Gallery, London, Galerie Bärbel Grässlin, Frankfurt and Friedrich Petzel Gallery, New York.

1

1 *Outsiderin*, 2002
Yellow ball-in-ball-
glass lamps, mixed
media, computer,
Internet connection
66 parts, 50 cm each.

2 *Seven Ends of
the World*, 2003
222 glass lamps.

4

3 *Outsiderin*, 2002
  Yellow ball-in-ball-glass
  lamps, mixed media, computer,
  Internet connection
  66 parts, 50 cm each.

4 *Montevideo*, 1999
  127 glass lamps,
  Internet computer link,
  computer unit, dimmer.

Tobias Rehberger

Louise Rice

Louise Rice is an artist fascinated by the complexities of the glass medium. Using mould blowing and *pâte de verre*, Rice describes her work as autobiographical but aims to negate the clichés that can often arise in the expression of personal feeling and observation in art.

Rice confounds accepted expectations of how glass should look and feel, creating works that have a universal familiarity while still being highly emotive:

> I hope to engage those who look at my work by taking familiar forms like objects from the domestic interior and transforming them, allowing them to bear the weight of intense emotional experience.

This is deftly communicated by the titles of her work, like *Safe as Houses*, 2003, a piece comprised by folded glass towels atop a weathered dresser, or *It's Alright, I'm Balanced Now*, 2003, a work which encompasses numerous sack-shaped glass vessels hanging from a wooden pivot, but less so in *Untitled*, 2004, for example, a floor installation of cotton reels and glass cylinders. The contradiction between the titles of such works and their composition is confusing as the relationship between the two is not always overtly clear. Other works, where objects are contained in glass vessels clearly speak of entrapment and limitation. As Rice states: "I tend to use colour quite sparingly in my work, relying more on form and texture to express meaning."

Rice's various influences include such prominent glass artists as Keiko Mukaide, Richard Price and Richard Meitner, all of who she has assisted throughout her career. She also founded a fully equipped hot glass studio at the Leitrim Sculpture Centre in Manorhamilton, the first of its kind in Ireland.

The artist is also involved in the Two Minds project, initiated by the Royal Society of Ulster Architects and Arts and Business Northern Ireland, which encourages collaboration between artists, as well as working as a glass designer for Caroline Dickson Architects.

1

2

1 *Untitled*, 2004
Cotton reels, glass.

2 *Cagey*, 2004
Wooden tools,
glass, mirror,
100 x 35 x 35 cm.

3 *Safe as Houses 1*, 2003
Glass, metal
cabinet, plaster,
150 x 90 x 40 cm.

4

4 *Attachment (cradle)*,
circa 2005
Glass, nylon,
45 x 25 x 7 cm.

5 *Attachment (tree pouch),*
  circa 2005
  Pâte de verre,
  30 x 30 x 5 cm.

Kiki Smith

American artist, Kiki Smith, is one of the most significant glass artists of her generation. She was born in Nuremburg, Germany, in 1954, after which her parents moved and settled in America; she now lives and works in New York. Recognised primarily for her sculpture, which she creates using a variety of media, such as wax, plaster and glass, Smith also considers her print work to be of vital importance to her art.

Often categorised as a 'feminist' artist, due to her emergence during the woman's movement in the 1970s, Smith displays a preoccupation with the female body in her work, which is infused with ideas of birth, regeneration, and sustenance. She often plays with erotic representations of women by male artists, as well as reworking myths and fairy stories, such as *Red Cap*, 2001,

based on *Little Red Riding Hood*, but with a feminist slant. Politically, Smith has made a great contribution to debate over issues such as AIDS, gender, race, and domestic violence.

After originally studying industrial banking in New Jersey, Smith moved to New York in 1976, where she met Charlie Ahearn, who introduced her to Collective Projects, an artist's collective. She became a key part of this group, producing radical and politically charged pieces of sculpture and installation.

Smith's work in glass took off in 1985, when she got involved with the New York Experimental Glass Workshop. Her work in glass often revolves around biological metaphors, magnifying the inner working of the body and bringing the private world of health and illness into the public arena.

She frequently displayed the body's organs (both human and animal), aiming to turn the body inside out (while at the same time maintaining a sense of aesthetic unity and composure, despite the violence of her subject matter). Her work in glass is often exhibited in a way that accentuates the fragility of the material, for example pieces are strewn across the floor of the gallery, inviting the viewer to step around them cautiously.

Smith received the Skowhegan Medal for Sculpture in 2000 and has participated in the Whitney Biennial three times in the past decade. Her work can be found in numerous prominent museum collections, including the Solomon R Guggenheim Museum, the Metropolitan Museum of Art, and the Museum of Contemporary Art, Los Angeles.

1

1 *Gang of Girls and Pack of Wolves*, 1999
   Fired paint on glass with brass and lead
   12 glass sheets 176.2 x 136.5 cm (each).
   Image courtesy of PaceWildenstein.
   Photograph by Ellen Page Wilson.

2 *Red Spill*, 1996
   Image courtesy of PaceWildenstein.
   Photograph by Shoshana Wane.

3

3 *Untitled (Eggs)*, 1996
Image courtesy of
PaceWildenstein.
Photograph by Joerg Lohse.

4 *Black Rain*, 1998
  Image courtesy of
  PaceWildenstein.
  Photograph by Ellen
  Page Wilson.

Kiki Smith

Kazue Taguchi

Kazue Taguchi is a New York-based, Japanese glass artist creating involving, temporary installations inspired by the colourful stained glass windows of old European Churches. "It was in the solemn churches that I first saw stained glass and my aesthetic awakening occurred", she explains.

Most of the windows I saw were figurative, but the projections they made on the wall and floors were abstract. To me these projections seemed like 'colour stains', that moved with the sun and the passing of time. The solemn environment of these old churches looked like a huge light installation to a young girl from a country where centuries old stained glass installations did not exist.

Her installations consist of cast, silk screened and painted glass, as well as reflective materials such as polyester foil and mirrors. Taguchi explores the magical play of reflections and shadows, truth and illusion, investigating the physical, philosophical and metaphysical qualities of the mirrored object.

"The relationship between my work and my interest in reflection is the most exciting part of my creative research", Taguchi claims.

Like sound, memory, feeling and imagination, light is intangible and invisible, but its effect on our lives is profound. My interest in creating works with light is in experiencing the phenomenon of their visual qualities as well as in the creation of a relaxing and sublime space.

Kazue Taguchi has undertaken studies at Joshibi University in Kanagawa/Japan, Fundació Centre del Vidre de Barcelona in Spain and at Virginia Commonwealth University in Richmond/America. She has received various grants and has exhibited widely in Europe, Japan and America. Her artworks are included in collections such as those of the Museo del Vidrio in Spain and the Moët & Chandon corporate collection.

1

1 *The Path to Hope*, 2006
Installation.

2&3 *Baby Sky Mountain
Travelling Series*, 2005
Photographed
mirror objects,
1,000 photographs.

2

3

Ione Thorkelsson

An essentially self-taught artist, the Manitoba-based Ione Thorkelsson has established a unique place for herself in the Canadian art scene. For over four decades, she has been exploring the physicality of glass, producing highly charged and technically demanding pieces. She has worked in different areas of glass art, from lampworking and glass-blowing to casting glass, in the most innovative and challenging ways. Through change and renewal, elements ever present in her work, Thorkelsson has constantly surprised audiences and unsettled expectations.

Her technique consists of mixing and heating raw materials such as silica sand, lime, soda and potash to very high temperatures and her cast installations can be seen in part as "a reaction against the glibly perfect licked surfaces of blown glass world". Thorkelsson finds in the lengthy and complex process of casting glass a new realm of emotional expressiveness not available in more spontaneous techniques.

In 2004, Thorkelsson created a major body of work called *Fragments and 2 partial reconstructions: everything we know about the Tropocene*. The piece is a collection of recovered fragments from an imagined, 'pseudo-paleontological' epoch, consisting of *surmoulage* constructions made out of found biological parts and structures.

Her most recent piece, *Ossuary: bones as signifiers of human absence,* is a thoughtful and challenging body of work. Her practice resonates with ambiguous meanings about death, contrasting bones as artefacts with bones as highly charged signifiers of human absence. Thorkelsson juxtaposes two experiences of death: the 'mass public death' taken from Gil Elliot's *The Twentieth Century Book of the Dead*, and a sense of individual, personal loss. Oscillating between opposites, between darkness and hope, between the personal and the collective, *Ossuary* is a subtle yet startling interpretation of humanity's attitude towards death.

Thorkelsson's work has been exhibited extensively in Canada, Europe, Hong Kong and America. In 1998 her comprehensive retrospective Unwilling Bestiary was exhibited at the Winnipeg Art Gallery in Manitoba. Her work is represented in various collections, including the Canada Council Art Bank; the Indusman Collection; the collection of Imperial Oil Canada; and the Massey Foundation Collection.

1

1 *Arboreal fragments*, 2004
  Cast glass, poplar, birch,
  ash, oak, plywood, quartz
  halogen lamp, 240 cm.
  Photograph by Robert Barnett.

2 *Matrix*, 2007
  Cast glass, steel, MDF board,
  240 x 240 x 116 cm.
  Photograph by David Barbour.

3 *Fragments and 2*
  partial reconstructions:
  everything we know about
  the Tropocene, 2004
  Photograph by Robert Barnett.

Eugenie Tung

Arriving in America from Hong Kong in 1995, Eugenie Tung was able to observe a wide slice of American life in the rural, suburban and urban communities in which she found herself. This exposure sparked her fascination with the way in which people live. "I have never stopped being curious about the human conditions that surround me", she says, "especially processes of change and how circumstances affect the decisions and choices we make, which inevitably lead to the different roads that we find ourselves on". Her work aims to capture that which is changing, ephemeral and transient in daily life, those recurring experiences and rituals that are both personal and universal and which, in their communality, unite us all.

More recently, Tung has explored the potential of glass in her work. A public arts project commissioned by the New York MTA Arts for Transit Program, *16 Windows* is located on an elevated railway platform in New York City. Featuring a series of glass panels similar in size to the real windows of buildings in the neighbourhood, it plays on the idea of the window as a screen through which we can observe the lives of others, which are so like our own. The various domestic activities shown centre around the working day and are divided into two categories—morning before the daily commute to work, and evening after the return journey—thus mimicking and evoking the daily rituals in the lives of those commuters passing by.

Tung's art has also been exhibited in Seattle, Washington; Portland, Oregon; San Diego; Madison, Wisconsin; Burlington, Vermont; Summit, New Jersey; and New York City, America. In 2007, her work was displayed as part of a group show, *The Photograph as Canvas*, at the Aldrich Contemporary Art Museum in Ridgefield, Connecticut, curated by Stephen Maine. In the same year, she was awarded the National Academy Abbey Mural Fellowship.

1

1&2 *16 Windows*, 2007
Fused glass in
platform windscreens.
122 x 75 cm per panel
(16 panels in total).
Commissioned by New
York Metropolitan
Transportation
Authority Arts for
Transit Permanent Art
Program. Glass panels
fabricated by Franz
Mayer of Munich, Inc.

Lucy Wade

An MA graduate from the Royal College of Art, Lucy Wade takes as her inspiration the natural world. Having spent her childhood on the Isle of Wight, Britain, she spends a considerable amount of time trying to capture, in two-dimensions, the environment—specifically water—that she encountered every day.

Wade uses the medium of glass to communicate something of the raw energy and unpredictability of water, leading to a preoccupation with the repetition that can by unearthed in such temporal elements as time, sound and movement. She explains:

I explore these ideas through the inherently repetitive processes of glassmaking. Hand crafted techniques give me the opportunity for an ongoing intimacy and sensitivity to the material.

The result of these investigations are such works as *Lines at the British Glass Biennale, 2004*, a four by four metre installation on brick in which stalactite-like drips of glass cascade in a vertical motion. Similarly inclined is *Lines at The Nicholls and Clark Building, London, 2005*, where the artist has installed a fountain-like wall of glass illuminated from behind, which captures both transparency of the medium and the moment at which the glass appears to be spilling over the top of the wall. Wade says of such works:

In contemplating the nature of glass in different states, observations are made about its qualities and ambiguities. I carefully choose processes that are sympathetic to the articulation of this diverse visual language to communicate a sensation or feature, intending traces of the process to be visible in the final form. Some are intensive and time-consuming, others gestural and spontaneous. Pieces therefore become precious for very different reasons.

Other works such as *Luse*, 2004, a glass slab on which glass shavings appear to have accumulated, hint at the very act of its production and indicate heightened, and almost obsessive, activity. *Crack*, on the other hand speaks of the very fragility of the medium itself. Such works "are determined as much by timing and the conditions in which they were made as by intention".

Wade's work has been shortlisted for numerous prizes and awards and has exhibited at the British Glass Biennale, 2005, the Minus One New London Glass at Designers Block, London and The Glass Sellers Prize, 2005.

1

1 *Now*, 2002
Hot-worked and flame-worked
glass, plasticine, light,
30 x 40 (with shadow) x 1.5 cm.

2 *Lines at the British Glass
Biennale*, 2004
Flame-worked glass on brick,
418 x 395 x 5 cm,
Photograph by Simon Bruntnell/
Muffled Visions.

Kate Williams

Kate Williams uses light in her glass-based designs and installations to reference elements from the natural world. Inspired by the transient nature of elemental forces and organic media, her site-specific light installations recreate naturally occurring forms, suspending them in both a situation and medium that encourage the viewer to reflect upon the relationship between art and nature.

Largely working in the technique of lamp-worked glass, this fluid and engaging practice helps influence the form of her sculptures. The resulting elongated and bulbous shapes demonstrate a playful aesthetic and approach to her craft, which is mirrored by the choice of cartoonish colours in works such as *Tame Triffids*, 2002, for example.

A recent collaboration with John Lloyd, in which she produced a series of kiln-cast power stations in uranium glass under-lit with ultraviolet light, is perhaps the clearest illustration of the tongue-in-cheek element that exemplifies her sculpture. Juxtaposing fears of nuclear waste, with the toxic green models of real power stations such as Sizewell in Suffolk, England and Doel in Belgium, alongside the nuclear power station's most famous pop-culture parody—Homer Simpson's Springfield, America—Williams uses the medium of glass to both highlight and mock conflicting attitudes to nuclear power.

Recent light installation commissions have seen Williams move away from the vivid colouration of her sculptural work to explore the subtle effects that result from the combination of natural and artificial media. A commission in 2001 for the Baltic restaurant saw Williams deploy illuminated fibre optics, with flints of amber suspended from cables, inducing variations in light and shadow as the cables and constellation of amber baubles move. Her two site-specific works, *Rain* and *Rainwave*, 2006, take the refractory potential of both water and glass to create a lighting installation that mimics and recreates the illusion of natural phenomena. Comprising water-filled glass droplets suspended from the ceiling by animated fibre optic cables, puddles of light are cast back onto the ceiling as the light from the cables is refracted through the glass and water.

1 *Blue Signature* (detail), 2004
Lass, argon,
wiring, transformer,
25 x 7 x 2 cm.

2 *Rain* (detail), 2005
Lamp worked glass,
water, fibre optics,
500 x 800 x 200 cm.

Artists Directory

Vessel/Object

Heike Brachlow: www.heikebrachlow.com

Matthew Curtis: www.axiamodernart.com.au

www.pismoglass.com www.rileygalleries.com

Suresh Dutt: www.sureshdutt.com www.sureshdutt.net

Anne Haavind: www.annehaavind.com

Kari Håkonsen: www.klartglass.no

Joseph Harrington: www.josephharrington.co.uk

Jamie Harris: www.jamieharris.com

Karl-Oskar Karlsson: www.karloskar.net

Jeremy Lepisto: www.travergallery.com/gallery_
artist_details/Jeremy-Lepisto.aspx

Ingrid Nord: www.nord-glass.no

Inge Panneels: www.idagos.co.uk

Jeffery Sarmiento: www.jsarmiento.com

Ethan Stern: www.ethanstern.com

Sculpture

Anne Brodie: www.annebrodie.co.uk

Stephanie Carlton-Smith: www.stephaniecarltonsmith.co.uk

Annie Cattrell: www.anniecattrell.com

Dale Chihuly: www.chihuly.com

Shirley Eccles: www.newburyarts.co.uk
www.greenham-common-trust.co.uk

Beth Lipman: www.bethlipman.com

Andrew Paiko: www.andypaikoglass.com

Angus M Powers: www.anguspowers.com

Minako Shirakura: www.minakoshirakura.com

Hanna Stahle: www.hannastahle.se

Surface/Light

Brian and Jenny Blanthorn: www.blanthorn.com

Bocci: www.bocci.ca

Lisa Cahill: www.lisacahill.com

Olafur Eliasson: www.olafureliasson.net

Anne Gant: www.gantglass.com

Michaela Nettell: www.michaela-nettell.com

Tanja Pak: www.tanjapak.com

George Papadopoulos: www.yorgosglass.com

Tom Pearman: www.tompearman.co.uk

Deborah Sandersley: www.deborahsandersley.com

Elaine Sheldon: www.sheldoncooney.com

Helen Tiffany: www.helentiffany.co.uk

Mark Zirpel: www.travergallery.com
www.bullseyegallery.com

Installation

Jeff Bell: www.glasscasts.co.uk

Richard Box: www.richardbox.com

Kirsty Brooks: www.kirstybrooks.co.uk

Nick Crowe: www.nickcrowe.net

Stuart Haygarth: www.stuarthaygarth.com

Mike Kelley: www.gagosian.com/artists/mike-kelley

Danny Lane: www.dannylane.co.uk

Silvia Levenson: www.silvialevenson.com

John Luebtow: www.luebtow.com

Katrin Maurer: www.katrinmaurer.com

Michael Petry: www.sundaramtagore.com
www.dbhbg.com www.westbrookgallery.com

Tobias Rehberger: www.haunchofvenison.com/en/
#page=home.artists.tobias_rehberger

Louise Rice: www.intoleitrim.com www.ccoi.ie

Kiki Smith: www.moma.org/exhibitions/2003/kikismith/

Kazue Taguchi: www.kazuetaguchi.com

Ione Thorkelsson: www.nord-glass.no

Eugenie Tung: www.eugeniestudio.com

Lucy Wade: www.lucywade.co.uk

Kate Williams: www.katewilliams.org

Acknowledgements

The editor wishes to thank Renee O'Drobinak, Mags Gainsford, Sophie von Oswald and Shama Khanna for their invaluable help with picture research, and Nikolaos Kotsopoulos, Aimee Selby, Kate Kilalea, Laura Barnicoat, Paul Teasdale, Diana Craig, Raven Smith and Nadine Monem for their insightful and stimulating profile texts. Thanks also to Matthew Pull for his uncompromising dedication to the project as well as his thoughtful and elegant design.

© 2008 Black Dog Publishing Limited,
London, UK, the artists and authors.
All rights reserved.

Black Dog Publishing Limited
10A Acton Street
London WC1X 9NG
United Kingdom

Tel: +44 (0) 20 7713 5097
Fax: +44 (0) 20 7713 8682
info@blackdogonline.com
www.blackdogonline.com

Edited by Blanche Craig at Black Dog Publishing.
Designed by Matthew Pull at Black Dog Publishing.

ISBN 978 1 906155 360

British Library Cataloguing-in-Publication
Data. A CIP record for this book is available from
the British Library.

Black Dog Publishing Limited, London, UK, is an
environmentally responsible company. *Contemporary
Glass* is printed on Sappi Magno Matt Classic, a
chlorine free FSC certified paper. Printed in Turkey

architecture art design
fashion history photography
theory and things

black dog
publishing
london uk

www.blackdogonline.com